# OORAH

## LEADERSHIP

## & TIP – OF – THE – SPEAR TRANSFORMATION

Michael J. Steele, Ed. D.

## "TIP OF THE SPEAR"

I AM THE "TIP OF THE SPEAR." I, AND I ALONE AM RESPONSIBLE FOR EXCELLENCE IN MY LIFE. I AM THE "TIP OF THE SPEAR", I AM COURAGEOUS, AND I TAKE ACTION. I AM PRINCIPLED AND ETHICAL. MY INTEGRITY IS UNWAVERING, AND MY MISSION IS CLEAR. I LEAD WITH A PASSION THAT IS CONTAGIOUS TO OTHERS, AND I ACCEPT NO EXCUSES FOR FAILURE IN MY LIFE, RELATIONSHIPS AND PROFESSION. THE "TIP OF THE SPEAR" MAKES THE SPEAR EFFECTIVE AND POWERFUL. I AM THE "TIP OF THE SPEAR" A SERVANT TO THOSE I LEAD AND FOLLOW. I LIVE A PURPOSEFUL LIFE, BECAUSE I CREATE MY PURPOSE, AND I HAVE COMPLETE CLARITY WHEN I SAY THAT LEADERSHIP IS ABOUT SERVING A PURPOSE GREATER THAN YOURSELF. I AM THE "TIP OF THE SPEAR" AND I WILL NEVER, EVER GIVE UP. I WILL STAND FAST WITH THE KNOWLEDGE AND POWER THAT MY EXCELLENCE DOES NOT COME WITHOUT HARDSHIP AND SACRIFICE.

– DR. MIKE STEELE

# Foreword

It was the summer of 2014. At the last minute, I had been called upon to act as the representative for Hamilton County at the Tennessee STEM Leadership Academy held in Nashville, TN. It would prove rather serendipitous that I would be at this particular STEM conference as I had just accepted a position at a new school in Chattanooga, TN. It was what they called a one-to-one school, so I felt it especially important that I learn as many new STEM practices as possible even though the school itself was not officially a STEM school in name, it seemed to be in practice.

There were many large group presentations but at some point, in the hubbub of the conference, we were given the opportunity as individual participants to go hear some smaller presentations from specific schools. One of these schools was Stratford STEM Magnet High School. Upon seeing this school listed I giggled a bit. I wasn't laughing because of the school, per say, but because my own mother had graduated from this school in the class of '79. I thought, "How funny! I can go see what my mother's alma mater is up to these days." So, I went, and I was absolutely blown away.

It certainly didn't hurt that the statistics I was hearing were truly impressive, gains upon gains in only 4 years' time. The school itself was a success story going from being a failing school to one that had a higher graduation rate than many schools of similar make-up and location. The school's turn-around was instrumental in creating a booming level of improvement in the neighborhoods surrounding the school. ...And at the helm was the presenter of this session and the executive principal of Stratford, Dr. Michael Steele.

      At this moment, I had very limited knowledge of this man other than what little I knew from the presentation and what I had heard from my (now) mother-in-law who was working in the cluster's enrollment office at the time. He carried himself with confidence as you would expect someone who was a former United States Marine or a principal of a thriving school, but something was different. The room was at rapt attention because in an hour presentation not only did we learn what amazing things were going on at his school, but we also gained insight into something else: a perspective into a leadership style that I, at least, had not seen before.

      After the presentation, I bee-lined it to Dr. Steele. I introduced myself by telling him, "I chose this session today because my mother graduated from your school years ago, my future mother-in-law thinks highly of the changes that have been taking place, and I hope you remember my name, because one day I'll likely move to Nashville to be closer to family and I'm going to work for you." After this monstrosity of a run-on sentence, Dr. Steele grinned, shook my hand, and asked, "Who is your mother-in-law?" Upon telling him, he asked how she was doing with her treatments. Even managing a school the size of Stratford, Dr. Steele knew exactly who I was talking about despite the fact she was an enrollment specialist who just happened to be stationed in his school. He knew she was undergoing treatments for breast cancer, and his concern was there rather than on the rest of my statement. I had told him that I was going to work for him one day, but the truth was I wasn't sure how that would come to fruition. He was over a high school, and my credentials were for grades 5-8. I thought of the logistics from time to time... Maybe I could get my algebra certification or something, but the truth of the matter was my heart was and still is in teaching middle schoolers, so I remained perplexed at how I would make good on this promise.

    The next two years were extraordinarily difficult for me. I was not met with the support I needed to thrive in the school that I had sought out in Chattanooga. I wasn't willing to call teaching quits, but I recognized the toll that my heart and mind were taking in my current placement. Additionally, after getting married, my spouse and I did want to move to be closer to our families. At Christmas of 2015, we announced to our families that we would be moving the coming summer. Amongst the shrieking of excitement and tears of joy, my mother-in-law pulled me to the side and said, "You know that Stratford is getting a middle school next year..." I looked at her in disbelief, and before the New Year even began, I started drafting emails to send to seek employment at Stratford.

    I haven't been disappointed. Dr. Steele talks about leadership, but he embodies it as well. He lets you know what you are expected to do. He praises a job well done. He lets you know if you need to do something else to improve. He says all the time, "When this school has a success it is yours. If there is a failure, I own that. It is mine." He gives credit and doesn't shy away from criticism. He pushes everyone to be the best version of themselves. He cares about the students and his staff. It is apparent in how he leads faculty meetings as well as in how he addresses teachers in one-on-one meetings.

I had a lot of healing and growing to do after the two years leading up to my beginning at Stratford. I had to learn how to trust leadership to lead me and learn how to trust myself to do the job I had been hired to do. I was never babied, never coddled, but somehow, I was pushed the right amount to feel a constant level of challenge that I could achieve and then work beyond. I owe a debt of gratitude to Dr. Steele for creating a culture that built a strong community within and beyond the walls of our school. I'm excited for his reach to extend even farther with the publication of this book.

- Brandi Fregoe, Teacher

## To My Readers...

Thank you for being curious, and courageous. I wrote this book, because for as long as I can remember, I've observed some terrific leadership from a few, and horrific leadership from most. When I think about those who did not lead with a compelling passion and vision it frustrated me, because they were entrusted to do so. I don't consider most too be bad people, I just learned over the years, they just are unsure how to lead, and then you have others who are not ethical in their life or leadership role. So, in my experience, having served in the Marine Corps, as a Deputy Sheriff, father, husband, brother and friend, and now an Executive Principal of a 5-12 public school, I wanted to share with everyone how it has worked for me and so many others personally, and professionally.

OoRah Leadership, is important to me, because when I joined the Marine Corps, I had nothing else. It was never my plan to join; it was out of desperation to find something in my life that was meaningful. No, my parents did not do a great job raising me or my siblings, but so what, it was what it was. I've never been the kind of person to make excuses, and joining and serving honorably in the Marine Corps taught me so much about leadership, and sacrifice. Now, I went to school for many years, sat in many classes, heard countless lectures on leadership, and honestly, I can't remember one professor who I feel got it right. Yes, they would lecture on servant leadership, transformational leadership, and so on, and on.

The entire time I asked myself, why do you have to identify with a particular style? Shouldn't all leaders understand that serving others first is their role? If I'm a transformation leader, does that mean I don't have to be great at service? Does the emotionally intelligent leader understand their weakness and strive to improve, or do they just identify with a leadership style, and carry on?

    I was a horrible high school student academically. I wish someone, just one adult in my school would have seen something in me besides athletic ability. I wish one adult would have encouraged me to write, read, or excel in something other than sports. I remember those adults who would encourage me to win the game, or make the catch, but I have no recollection of any "leader" at my school, taking time to encourage me academically, spiritually or emotionally. My youth pastor, Robin Kuder, and my oldest brother Joe, were the only consistent men in my life that ever encouraged me to be better than I was. So, over the years, I became fascinated with leadership, and what authentic leadership really looks like. There are literally a million books on leadership, and I've tried to read a lot of them. I'm fascinated with how to lead myself, and others towards winning, growing, caring, and loving. I'm also fascinated when I see teams being led by most who do not understand that their leadership is 100% about people, and not a bottom line. Yes, the bottom line matters, but how you get there with amazing people also matters. I tell my staff all the time, if our academic progress improves greatly this year, but my team hates coming to work, I failed as their leader. Yes, many would just be happy with the final results, never considering the unbelievable sacrifice an entire team made. Some leaders would not even celebrate their team, or acknowledge any milestones.

I've traveled all over the United States, and I've even had several opportunities to share OoRah Leadership with the St. Lucian police force, and Sandals Resorts in the Caribbean. The feedback I get is just unreal, and I don't think it is just me, but how we dissect what loving leadership, OoRah Leadership looks like. There has never been a time that my team and I presented OoRah Leadership where several wouldn't come up in tears, because they have been seeking the answers that we all seek. How can I feel alive, safe, proud, ethical, happy, joyful, and loving? And, although we all have times we don't feel any of these things, there is a way to live your life where you can experience this and more, but you must want it. You must want it so bad that you are willing to be honest about you. I chose "OoRah" because I learned that there are no limitations in leaders, or there should not be. I had one of my leaders tell me that she was not good at expressing her appreciation or genuine concern for others, although she really does appreciate them and is concerned for them. I told her I appreciated her own self-evaluation and understanding of her weaknesses, but then told her that she is going to have to improve if she wanted to reach a level of excellence in her life and leadership role. I expect my entire team, especially those in leadership roles to demonstrate all aspects of leadership, and to be constantly working on those areas identified as weaknesses. I accept no excuses for not trying because there are no excuses for not trying. So, I created a leadership model, and called it OoRah Leadership. No, it is not based on the Marine Corps, but it certainly was inspired by the Corps.

I wrote this book to share with you how we used OoRah Leadership to transform Stratford High School, which was once one of the most dangerous schools in Tennessee, and was in the midst of state takeover when I was hired. After our first year, Stratford was taken off the list of being dangerous, and was no longer being considered for state takeover. Over the past seven years we've grown our graduation rate from 59% to 86.2%, which is 5% higher than our district average, and the culture and environment is fantastic. We serve over one thousand students every day, 87% of which are on free and reduced lunch. Our student population is also approximately 87% impoverish-minority students, so I don't like hearing excuses about how this can't be done. Stratford's transformation has changed the entire East Nashville community, a community which was once considered undesirable, and is now thriving with new homes, and businesses. East Nashville is now one of the most popular places to live in Nashville, because parents know they can send their children to an outstanding public school.

You can change whatever it is that is holding you back, and you can transform your team, but I can assure you that this journey is not always easy, and you will be confronted with what you need to change about you. Read this book, and then reach out to me and let me help you on this journey that so many others have taken.

Me and my amazing grandson, A.J.
This little boy has Pop Pop's heart.

# OoRah Encouragement

"Seven years ago, when I first met Dr. Steele, I was an unlicensed teacher, I weighed over 359 lbs., had six children with the same amazing woman, but was unmarried, and I was drifting. Dr. Steele introduced me to OoRah Leadership, and he not only held me accountable, but has supported and mentored me every step of the way. OoRah Leadership does not accept excuses, even if you have a good one, don't be seduced by an excuse. I've lost over 150 lbs., got certified, and now serve as an assistant principal. I married that amazing woman, and made my family real. OoRah Leadership, and Dr. Steele were the driving force in my transformation. In August 2017, I graduated with my doctorate degree.

As a black man, I never imagined that a white man could be my mentor, but as Dr. Steele says often, "There is no place in OoRah Leadership for not wanting to inspire and support every person who wants to find excellence and joy." I hope those of you who are struggling with life and success goes on this journey, and I also hope that principals will understand that they can lead a transformation of any school."

- Vincent Jones, Assistant Principal, Stratford STEM School

"I've worked in education for over 30 years and Dr. Steele is one of the best motivational speakers I have ever heard. I've rarely seen someone that cares so much for everyone, but has the ability to hold them to the highest standards while the entire time building meaningful relationships. Dr. Steele has a passion for minority and underprivileged children, and his insight and ability to mentor is remarkable."

- Maurice Fitzgerald, Head Football Coach, Stratford STEM School

"Dr. Steele's presentation on leadership was the best I've ever heard. He makes you want to change and forces participants to take a very close look at what is keeping them from being excellent, not only at their jobs, but in life."

- Jon Stephens, FBI Special Agent, Retired

"OoRah Leadership is unlike any other leadership practice or model. OoRah Leadership does not allow excuses or prejudice to interfere with what is good and fair for all people. We use OoRah Leadership to transcend what it means to love all people, and expect excellence every day. OoRah Leadership confronts you to be true about yourself, and how you are getting in the way of you."

- Brittany Edmonson, Attorney

## Acknowledgements/Dedication

I want to thank my beautiful wife Joyce and my amazing family for the inspiration to write this book. You all believed I could do this long before I believed in myself. Over the past 30 years I have tried my damnedest to be an honorable man, who walks daily with integrity. I have worked hard, helped numerous people, made mistakes, learned from those mistakes, and made more mistakes. Through every success, and every mistake you all have been by my side, loving me, making me laugh, holding me accountable and inspiring me to always be better.

Joyce, I've loved you from the very first date. You have been such an amazing rock of strength over the years. You have always supported me no matter what I wanted, going back to school, moving around the country, conference trips, and even those times when I chose to sing karaoke. I love you with all I know, and I'm proud to be your husband. I dedicate this book to you, and I hope that you will always know that you are the most amazing wife and mother.... ever.

My wonderful children, Mariel, Zak, Mikaylee, and Ella Grace. God has certainly blessed your mother and me beyond what we deserve. You are all amazing, and it makes me very proud to be your father. I have tried so hard to live a life of character, and to set a good example for each of you. You all know I had to write this book, because each of you at some point have made fun of me for not having started it already, so I went for it. I love each of you so much, and I hope that when you think of me, you know that I loved you enough to hold you accountable, teach you, and inspire you.

My amazing brothers and sisters......wow we survived and have all led very productive and for the most part harmonious lives. I love each of you, and draw inspiration from you as well. In this book, I will talk about things that I remember, or feel that I endured to hopefully shed light on who I am today, and where I glean ideas. It is truly amazing how close we are, everything considered. I hope you are proud of this book, and please know that I did my best to just speak from the heart in the hopes that I would be able to encourage and help others.

My students, friends, colleagues, don't ever be afraid. Don't ever be afraid to do what you know is blameless and good. Courage ignites our passions, and makes us more focused. I have learned so much from all of you, and my only wish is that you live a life of integrity where helping others find hope is your priority. I hope that I have honored each of you, living a life of character and integrity. I hope that I have never let any of you down because I was not walking the talk. My students, all of you, former, present and future, I love you. Yes, I said that, and I promise you will not hear that very much in your professional lives, and perhaps you have not heard that much in your personal lives, but I think about the power of that statement all the time, and I want you to know that truer words have never been spoken. Learn to love others, no matter where they come from, or where they have been. Learn what true love really looks like, and how to grow it. Thank you all for being an inspiration to me, yes, even those of you who made me work harder.

    Mom, I love you, and I wish you were still here to see what you started. Your children have done wonderful things, embraced so many, helped many more and inspired hope. Your grandchildren are amazing, and your legacy for being a mom who demonstrated love, even when she may have had limited understanding or vision, is solid. You are a part of all my happiness, sadness, success and failure, but I would not have it any other way. You defended me no matter what, and you provided for us. I forgave you long ago, and I love you.

"Your leadership journey begins with you. Serve those you are blessed to lead, and make them your priority. The moment you waiver from the people you lead, is the moment your peace and joy start to fade. It's all about the people. Be dynamic and authentic with everyone."

– Dr. Mike Steele

21

## Understanding Myself, and My Journey

The question of "why" has come up numerous times over the past few years, and I have spent a lot of time pondering it. Why not? What can my words possibly mean to others who may be living a life without purpose or not finding happiness and joy on their journey? So, I've come to the conclusion that my experiences have brought me on my journey through many valleys, mountain tops, and every other place in between. Read this book, and challenge yourself daily to make this journey the most epic of all time. Be confronted with what you need to change, celebrate, overcome, endure, and survive every day, so that you have power and control over the journey you are on.

Another reason "why" is because there are way too many "leaders" out there who are not doing it right, and in the process, are hurting others. Most leaders just don't know how to lead. They are great people, and want to love and inspire others, but they either don't have the courage, or simply don't know how to do it. For example, I recently interviewed for a promotion within my district, but was not offered the position. When I received feedback, I laughed so hard. The positive feedback I received was that my passion was obvious, and that I had great confidence in myself. Some of the "wonderings" were that "will he intimidate others, and how will his passion be perceived?" You see, this is what this book is all about. This book is about how you can overcome the hypocrisy of poor and failed leadership, create a life of purpose, a career of excellence, and build relationships that are powerful and rewarding.

Who am I? This book is dedicated to discovering who you are. For me, it would be a journey of unbelievable memories, worries, excitement, fear, love, pain... the things we all experience, and that shape who we are. Everyone, especially leaders and organizations need to be able to answer two essential questions:

Who am I, and who do I want to be?

Answering the question of, "who am I" requires a great deal of honesty and self-reflection. It is not easy to take an in depth look at yourself and find those things that you don't like or need to change. And to answer the question of "who do I want to be" can take a lifetime. I am still striving to be certain of things, and I will never stop striving. I've always wanted to be a great husband and father, and for the most part believe I have accomplished that; you would have to ask my wife and children. Now, I want to be an amazing grandfather, and author. I want to continue helping others find success in their personal and professional lives. I want to continue traveling and motivating organizations and leaders to strive for excellence. My childhood offers a great insight of who I am, and what motivated me to want to be a leader of immense character and integrity.

I was born in Boston, Massachusetts, but raised in Florida. I have very little recollection of my childhood, and I'm certain that has a lot to do with the uncertainty of my safety and security growing up. I remember moving around a lot and being exposed to some, not so great places. I have five sisters, and two brothers, and only one of my brothers is from the same father. You can start to imagine how dysfunctional our family was growing up, but I must say how proud I am of my siblings for surviving, overcoming, and creating wonderful lives. As I understand it, my father basically ran out on us when I was just a baby, and I have no memory of him living with us. I had no idea how my upbringing would shape the man you see today, but I am thankful for it. I won't go as far to say, "I wouldn't change a thing", but it certainly makes me think from time-to-time how things could have been different. For the most part, I think of how blessed I was, and am to have survived, many others are not as blessed, and I make sure to never forget that, especially when I'm working with children.

    My mother was married several times throughout my childhood, and as I look back I not only understand why this was necessary, but forgive any circumstances her marriages may have caused. We have no choice but to overcome hurt, and disappointment in our lives. Now, I realize it is easier said than done, but the truth is, you will either overcome it, and create hope and joy, or you won't. Although I use to have plenty of baggage, and probably still do, I was confronted with the choice to overcome or endure. I was confronted with the choice to want more or to live a predetermined life. I was confronted with growing, learning, leading and excelling, or following in the footsteps of so many men I should have been able to count on, instead their selfishness, and deceit led them down of a path of regret, and shame. I always knew from an early age that I wanted to be a great husband, father, friend, and leader. Perhaps I'm one of those people who just say, "I can do it, because you said I can't."

Being transparent has never been a problem for me, and from time-to-time, it has not always been the best choice for me, but this must be said. My brother Bobby is two years older than me, and growing up, he was my hero. I remember going to sleep almost every night so scared, that unless he was with me, I never slept. Of course, we had to sleep in the same bed, so I would wait for him to fall asleep, and I would just push my leg over just enough to feel his leg. I wanted to make sure that if he got up, I would also wake up. It's a terrible thing living in fear. As we got older, and as things improved for us, Bobby did not want to sleep in the same bed, and he certainly did not want me touching him. I'm not sure when that stopped, but I'm so grateful for my brother, Bobby, and how he helped me be the person I am today.

Honestly, as fathers go, I had no role model or teacher. Let me just say that my fathers did not share the same vision I have about what an amazing father looks like or should be. Many of you, I'm certain understand what I'm talking about. Because I did not live with my biological father, I did not get to see him very often. My brother, Bobby and I would visit in the summers, and I don't think either of us really understood all the implications of going away for the summer, but we would board a plane and fly to Atlanta to spend time with our father, and his new family. Now and then, I reflect on those summer visits, and I know my father must have regretted all the missed opportunities to teach, and inspire us. I know I want to always be an inspiration to my family, especially my children. Our step-father was certainly very interesting to say the least, and I certainly do not want to disparage him in any way, but telling the truth about that time in my life is certainly necessary to frame the father and husband I am today. Our step-father, as I'm told, was not an educated man, but growing up, he seemed so smart. Of course, I don't consider being educated as just having a college degree. When thinking about being an amazing father, I first think about being an amazing husband. Yes, I'm aware that you can be an amazing single parent, I know many, but for me however, I felt that it was extremely important. I regret that I can't think of a characteristic or inspiration that my step-father gave me. To this day, I have no understanding of why he treated me different than others, and I understand that some of my siblings have an entirely different perspective, which I respect.

Whenever my step-father would get angry, which seemed often, he would go into the bedroom for days at a time. He would not come out of that room for days, or until we had all gone to bed. His inability to assess and analyze his anger or disappointment was nonexistent, so all of us had to be afraid of what he would say or do when he finally decided to come out of hiding. Most of the time, when he would finally emerge, it was like nothing had ever happened, and that the world was a great place again. I remember one time, I was being annoying to my sisters, and they told on me. My step-father called me over, and with an open hand slapped me across the face. He hit me so hard that I thought I was going to pass out. You see, this book is about truth, life and leadership. This book is about either helping you or confronting you....I hope it does both, and that it inspires you to seek a better understanding of joy and excellence.

In twenty-five years of marriage, I have never yelled at my wife in anger, called her bad names, and I've certainly never put my hands on her. I have never hit my children anywhere, but their ass, and oh how thankful I am that I did, because we have four amazing, respectful, hard-working children, who I know will be able to survive in this world. Men, you have such amazing power and ability. You have the power to influence your entire family, and you were created to powerfully influence your family. You were made to protect, defend and honor your wife, and children. Remember, when you come home, no matter what kind of day you are having, they need you to come home ready to lead, honor, and protect them. Your family needs you to love and inspire them. You, dad, husband, are usually the creator of the atmosphere in your household. Don't be that man who is unwilling to grow towards being the greatest husband and father you can be. I promise you, one day, you will be so thankful you worked so hard to be a better man.

You might say, "So I can't have a bad day?" The truth, of course you can, but your bad day does not have to deflate, or scare your family. I have bad days, and disappointments, and from time-to-time I am more quiet than usual, because I'm thinking, but I do not take it out on my family…they deserve so much more than for me to not be able to acknowledge and understand how I'm feeling. They deserve someone who would never mistreat them, no matter what. When I speak at conferences, people often ask me how I do it, and here is what I tell them.

- I first recognize my attitude. Before I go inside or allow my mood to impact my family, I do everything I can to recognize why I'm feeling a certain way. Now, this is going to be difficult for some of you because you have never seen this growing up with your own fathers, and it takes a continual learning process to keep it in check. You see, no one is perfect, and you may not be able to maintain this all the time, but if you are willing to be a life-long learner, then you have a great chance of changing. You must decide if being a loving husband and father is important to you. You must choose now to be the man of character and integrity your family deserves. There are no excuses for making your family feel fear, intimidation or uncertainty. Be the man you should be.
- Self-talk. I talk myself through what is going on, and I say to myself, "Before you walk in that house, you need to know that how you are feeling does not need to impact those you love in a negative way." Yes, you can have bad day, and yes, you can just not be yourself every now and then. When I recognize that I may not be able to overcome, I tell my wife and children, I explain to them that I may be in a quiet mood, or I may just want to be

alone. They always support and appreciate knowing that they did not do anything to create this for me. I can assure you, my wife and children know very well about my upbringing because as I've learned more about myself, I have shared with them how I'm feeling. These are the most wonderful people in your life, and you must make it a mission to be their warrior.
- I intentionally and purposefully speak with my wife and children about life, and how I'm feeling. So, many parents don't talk with their children or each other about who they are, and what makes them who they are. My children have seen me cry numerous times, but I know so many men who think this a weakness. I will tell you, the weakness is yours. Powerful is the man or leaders who can show their emotions, and have others not only understand, but respect them.
- I apologize. When I'm wrong and sometimes even when I don't think I'm wrong, I apologize to my family for simply being in a foul mood, and having a bad attitude. Let me tell you parents and men, a few things that are very powerful for your family and children. First, make sure your children see you loving each other. Don't keep your love a secret from them. I grab my wife all

the time and dance with her, kiss her and sometimes just make out, and I want my children to see it. I also apologize when I need to. When your children see you strong and consistent, that is what they expect, but when they see you vulnerable and willing to say, "I'm sorry" then you are really exploring powerful, inspirational and meaningful growth. I learned a lot from my step-father, and there were times when he was nice, and fatherly. But men, you can't be loving, kind, ethical occasionally, it should be, and needs to be a life-long journey. Your leadership needs to always be authentic, courageous, and caring.

My brother Joe is several years older than me, and if there ever was a man that demonstrated authenticity, courage, and caring, it was Joe. Joe is my mentor, even when he had no idea. When I was in the seventh grade, we moved from Orlando, Florida to Tallahassee. Throughout the years, my brother Bobby and I would spend a few weeks with Joe and his amazing wife, June. Although Joe and June had no children at the time, Joe took to being a father figure so easily. During our visits, everywhere Joe went, he took us with him. He took us golfing, to play basketball, and to church. He demonstrated daily what a loving and caring husband looked like, and he had the courage to take us to church. To this day, I remember that my brother Joe never forced his beliefs on us, but it was obvious that what he had was special.

Following our move to Tallahassee, our mother used to watch Joe and June's son, Jeffrey. It was awesome coming home and spending time with Jeffrey before he was picked up. Let me just say for the record, I have some amazing nieces and nephews, and they all love their uncle Michael…as they should. Every time Joe or June would come to pick up Jeff they were always so excited to see him, and to see each other after having been apart for the day. Joe was a banker and always dressed so sharp. I'll always remember that he carried a gold pen in his pocket, and I thought that it was the epitome of success. I also saw how Joe treated his wife June with respect, honor and love, and I knew then that I wanted to do the same. By the way, as soon as I could I bought a gold pen, and have it on me most days. It is amazing how symbolic a gold pen can be, but for me it represented everything I wanted to start off being. We all have reasons or excuses why we are not happy or successful. We align with those who love, understand or at least put up with us, and we start creating a life. Sometimes, the journey we start after high school is drastically different and unexpected with regards to how we were raised, and then there are other times where one just continues with the family legacy of either being happy and successful, or not.

When I was in the ninth grade I visited a church with my girlfriend, which also happened to be the Christian school she attended. After the service, a large man came up to me and asked me where I attend school. He then proceeded to tell me that he was the football coach and asked me if I was interested in coming to school there and playing football for him. Of course, I was flattered, and since my girlfriend was already attending this nice-private school, I thought, why not? As I've looked back over the years I must laugh because my parents never came to the school, made a phone call or seemed to care that I was changing schools, and that this man was taking care of everything. Of course, being so young, I had no idea of all that was involved in this decision, and how it would impact my life. I guess I was just thankful and flattered that I was asked to play, having no idea about any ethical implications.

So, I started going to school, playing football and attending church at my new school. Of course, I came into this entirely new environment feeling cared for, and respected. I would eventually learn that caring about me or demonstrating ethical leadership was not always the priority for many of the adults I would encounter. After my first year I had a reasonably successful football season, broke up with my girlfriend, met someone else, and just observed my surroundings. My parents mainly remained disconnected, and not really involved in my schooling or extra-curricular activities. As long as I was home at a decent hour, they never said anything. Looking back, I not only think they should have been entirely more involved in my education and activities, but they should have been much more aware of the things and people in my life. No, I'm not feeling sorry for myself, I just know that a great parent is immersed in the lives of their children…or they should be.

Over the course of my high school years, at this private-Christian high school, I learned a great deal about character, integrity, and faithfulness.

From some adults, I considered it authentic, but it pains me to say that I learned much more about the adults who were supposed to be ethical, courageous and faithful, but were anything but. It is far too easy to disappoint, hurt, and sacrifice others instead of being consistent, loving, ethical, and truly faithful. Let me just say that I met a lot of adults when I was a child who were portraying a life of character, and faith, but really cared little about that and more about what made their lives better. Yes, I stayed and graduated, barely, and later found out that my coach had some serious personal issues that explained a lot about his behavior. I will say that his wife, my teacher, was a wonderful woman and teacher, and to this day I am thankful for her leadership, and mentoring. She was a very genuine and loving teacher, and never let me get away with anything. I am mindful, however, that every time she disciplined me, which was often, she always made it a point to restore my spirit when the time was right. You never know when that person will come along, so do not hesitate to learn from anyone, and don't miss opportunities to impact the lives of others as often, and intentional as possible.

    I was an above average football player, and was recruited by some small schools. Of course, when you are in high school every college sends you letters, so when I started getting letters from Florida State, Nebraska, I thought I was much better than I really was. As my senior year came to an end I noticed that I had no scholarship offers, even though a few colleges, including the University of Central Florida had already given me a verbal commit. I would find out later that my football coach called Central Florida and told them

I was not interested, he did the same to one of my teammates. To this day I still have no idea why he did that, and although everything turned out fine, this is a perfect example of how adults demonstrate a lack of character, and put their own needs first. It is truly amazing how some adults will treat children, never understanding that those children will grow up to remember their unethical behavior, and demonstration of no leadership. Leadership is an interesting word, but what does it mean to have leadership or to be a leader? Does anyone really know? Let's dive into that later, but yes, there is a life of leadership that can be overwhelming inspirational and rewarding.

      I graduated from high school, to the surprise of my entire family. If you could see my transcripts, you would see that I was not the most studious student in the world, but sometimes, you just have to figure things out instead of trying to be perfect and please everyone around you. So, I got very good at figuring things out in my childhood, as did all my siblings. I would say that we are a family who knew how to, "figure things out, and survive", but now what?

      Let's face it, even if I had a scholarship offer, I was in no way ready to go to school, do the work, study and succeed. I could barely write a paper, much less go to class and pass college exams. I had no idea what I wanted to do, or could be successful doing. When you graduate from high school you are supposed to have a plan of sorts, or at least you should have been presented with options. Well, there was one option for me.

One day during music class a young man walked into our room. I had never seen anyone look as sharp, or walk with such intention and meaning. I mean he owned that classroom the moment he walked in, and no one could take their eyes off him. His name was Staff Sergeant (SSgt.) Robby Winchester, United States Marine Corps. SSgt. Winchester spoke with our entire class for about an hour, and he captured our attention the entire time. Standing there in his dress blue uniform he talked about opportunities, and travel. He spoke about promotions and education, but he said one thing that grabbed my attention, and to this day I still remember. He said, "If you join the Marine Corps, just remember that you will be the best, are expected to remain the best, and will live your entire life with a new mission of leadership, integrity and honor. You will learn how to kill, but may not have to. You will learn how to save lives, but may not have to. You will learn to lead others with a compelling vision that their needs always come before your own. The United States Marine Corps is the finest fighting force in the world, and we only want the best." WOW! I left class speechless, which is a rare thing for me. I couldn't stop thinking about what he said, but I still had this unrealistic dream of playing college football. It would be a while before I would see SSgt. Winchester again. Little did I know that he would be the reason I started this amazing journey of leadership, and honor.

One day after graduation I walked to the campus of Florida State University, and even went in to speak with a financial aid counselor. She went over everything I needed, made a plan, and was very encouraging. I left entirely overwhelmed with the vast information that was shared. Immediately it occurred to me that I had no idea who my high school counselor was, and I certainly had never had anyone speak with me about not only going to college, but registering, paying for and succeeding at the next level, so I walked back home dejected and uncertain about my future. Yes, I was scared because in this world, especially now, if you don't have a plan you can literally disappear while others go on. Trust me, I've seen it growing up, and with people I love. That is why as a high school principal, I am adamant that my counselors meet with their students' numerous times throughout the year. I expect them to build meaningful and purposeful relationships, and to start helping our students think about the future. I expect my administrators to do the same, because I do the same.

A few days later, I woke up around 10am, laid in bed for a while, and wasted time. I remember my thoughts of fear, and uncertainty. I remember thinking about my future, and not having a plan, not even for the very next day. So, I got out of bed, got dressed and started walking. I remembered driving by the Marine Corps recruiting office, so I started walking in that direction. I remember, it seemed like ten miles, but, it was only about six. Still a long walk, but what else did I have to do. I had no idea if it was the same office where SSgt. Winchester worked, but I was hoping to speak with him.

True story, when I arrived at the office, SSgt. Winchester was walking out with another young man. He recognized me because I was friends with his sister. I explained that I wanted to speak with him about joining the Marine Corps, and he said, "OUTSTANDING!" He said he was on his way with the other young man to take the armed services vocational aptitude battery (ASVAB) test, and asked me if I wanted to go as well. Of course, I was excited, and remember not being nervous at all. SSgt. Winchester was awesome, and a role model for all Marines and recruits. We drove to the Post Office, took the test and then returned to the recruiting office. All-in-all, it took about three hours, and when we returned I received my scores. Let me just say, again, my transcripts told a compelling story about my test-taking ability. Also, let me just say that my scores did not support my candidacy to be a pilot or doctor.

During our time together, we talked about the Marine Corps, service, honor and all sorts of wonderful things. I was hooked, not so much because I was eager to dive into this difficult world, but for me, at the time, it was something very few were doing, and something I'm certain no one thought I could accomplish. This meeting happened on a Tuesday, and by Friday I was at the medical station in Jacksonville, Florida. I spent three days in Jacksonville and on the third day, boarded a train to Savannah, Georgia. I never spoke with my parents or family about my decision to join the Marine Corps. I never told my mother I was leaving for boot camp. Usually, going to boot camp never happens this fast, and today it can take months to start boot camp. I am so thankful that I never had time to consider it, or have someone try to talk me out of it. I promise you, there are people who love you, yet they will still try to talk you out of something that is good for you, not because they are concerned, but because they don't want to be confronted with their own lack of courage, and dedication. I joined the United States Marine Corps, and I never looked back. I had no idea what I was doing, or what was going to happen. I knew nothing about war, or service, and I knew less about leadership or sacrifice; those things that make us great leaders. I knew nothing about Semper Fi (Always Faithful) or OoRah!!! And, I certainly never imagined that I would one day introduce OoRah Leadership to so many people and organizations. We are all learning every day, and we must always be mindful that we have something powerful to offer to others, even if it is only a word of encouragement.

*"Human beings are selfish. You and I are selfish. A defining moment in your life will be when you can recognize when you are being selfish, and consider others before considering yourself."*

~ Dr. Mike Steele

## My OoRah Leadership Roots

"OoRah" is a Marine Corps word to acknowledge success, motivation, excellence and grit. Whenever we thought the work was getting too hard, we would shout, "OoRah" to each other, and like an echo you would hear "OoRah" all the way down the line. "OoRah" simply signifies that excellence is expected, and that no matter how challenging your life or situation gets, everything is going to be fine as long as you never, ever quit. So, years later, after having attended numerous leadership courses, and certifications, I concluded that I wanted to create my own leadership model. I did this because I do not believe you should get to choose a leadership model, and only be responsible for the specifics of that model. On my journey, I've seen way too many leaders paint themselves into a corner when it comes to leadership. As a leader, you are not excused from not being excellent in all aspects of leadership. When leaders say they are "transformational" leaders, and never mention service, sacrifice, and love when describing their leadership traits, I believe that allows them to rationalize why they are not highly competent in all areas of leadership.

OoRah Leadership does not accept excuses for failure. You are expected to be highly capable in all areas of leadership, not just a select few. You might say that you are not good at expressing your feelings with others, well get better, because those who are following you need you to be at least competent to meet their needs, and leadership is all about inspiring and meeting the needs of those who follow. The entire premise of leadership is that you are always willing to grow, learn, and evolve, so when you realize what you need to change or create, then do it without excuses, rationalizations, or hesitation. It takes courage to change, or admit you need to change, and I guess that is why, so many people hesitate, or never do. What do you have to lose by changing your life or your leadership practices? When is the last time you felt inspired about your life, and what was going on in your world? More importantly, when is the last time you've inspired others by the way you are living your life?

In January of 1984, I arrived at Parris Island, South Carolina. Now, Parris Island is a small island tucked away just outside Beaufort, SC, and not too far from Hilton Head Island, an amazing tourist destination. When new recruits arrive on the island, the receiving Marines intentionally wait until the middle of the night to drive you on base. Parris Island is not that big, but driving us on in the middle of the night is disorienting, so it discourages anyone from trying to escape boot camp, and believe me, some tried. After a dark tour of the island, the bus pulls up to a building and a very sharp Marine gets on the bus, and from the moment he started speaking, my life would change forever. He said, "When I tell you, you will get off the bus as quickly as you can! You will not talk, look around or eye ball me whatsoever! Do you understand?" Of course, I can't remember everything he said, and I know it was much more colorful, but you get the picture.

My life as I knew it was over, and I had to decide to never quit or to surrender. In life people quit all the time. I've seen way too many people quit on the things that were so good for them. I've seen people quit simply because they had no character, grit, or OoRah Leadership in their lives. I've seen people quit because they did not have the mental toughness to endure, and I've seen people quit because they were simply sorry. On the other hand, I've seen people work through so much pain and fear to conquer the mission, and never quit. And, I knew those who gave their lives and sacrificed everything because they would never quit. It's all about never quitting, and continuing to push forward even when you feel like there is no reason to try or chance of success. You are going to fail, feel pain, and regret, but there is no regret like surrendering, and admitting that you don't have what it takes.

     When I got off the bus I noticed yellow footprints painted on the road. The drill instructor very loudly ordered us to find a set of footprints and get on them. Well, of course we did not get off the bus fast enough, so we were ordered back on, which went on for a good thirty minutes. We all would later learn that this form of harassment was intentional, and so meaningful if you wanted to live your life as a Marine. The drill instructors kept us awake for about two days, and in that time, we got our first haircut, all our shots, our clothing and they even marched us into this large room full of showers and instructed us on how to properly bathe. Everything we did for the duration of boot camp was by design. Our first shower was in freezing water, which lasted about an hour, because we had to have permission to wash, and if we washed without permission, we were punished. It did not matter if we were cold or tired. It mattered less that we all had so much soap in our eyes. I was in the United States Marine Corps, and I was either going to survive and be better for it, or quit, and quitting was not an option. I kept thinking to myself that these few days of torture were getting me closer to graduation, but little did I know that these days of "receiving" do not count toward your actual training days.

    I never informed my parents that I joined the Marine Corps. The first they learned of it was when they received my first letter from Parris Island, and that letter only said that I had arrived and was doing well. When my mother got that letter, she wrote back, and the very first thing she said was, "Son, what have you done? There is no way you will make it. "I was not surprised by my mother's letter, because I really don't have much recollection of my parents being encouraging at all. Growing up, my parents were more concerned with how we were going to survive, so there wasn't a lot of time or money for music lessons, and vacations. I wish to this day I had kept the letters I received, they motivated me then, and I'm certain could still provide motivation now.

    At some point, we finally got to sleep, but couldn't because we knew that the very next day we were meeting our drill instructors. I started off in 3rd Battalion which is considered by many harder than the others, but it's not, it's was just more isolated than the others. Meeting your drill instructors for the first time is an experience you will never forget. You are sitting there with about 80 other bald men, nervous of the unknown, excited for what could be, and yes, scared. Then walked in the sharpest, fittest and meanest looking men you can imagine. We had three drill instructors and one senior drill instructor, who is supposed to be like the "nice one," but whatever, he wasn't. After a short speech from the senior drill instructor, he turns to the other drill instructors and says, "Drill instructors, turn these recruits into Marines." From that moment on all hell broke loose and the journey begins. As you can imagine there is a lot of yelling and commands, and there is no way you are going to be able to do anything right, so you just do what you are told in the moment. On that first day, I was made a squad leader, and I thought that my choice to join was totally solidified. Within 20 minutes I had been fired from squad leader and sent to the back of the platoon. This would happen to me about 20 times on and off throughout boot camp.

After meeting our drill instructors, one of the first things we did was to take the physical fitness test (PFT). When I joined the Corps, I was in what I thought was good shape, and all you really needed to do was to be able to do some pull-ups, sit ups, and run three miles. Well, I found out quickly that although I could do the minimum pull ups and sit ups, I could not do the run within acceptable limits. Prior to joining the Corps, I had never run more than a mile, much less three. So, within just a few days, I would face my first challenge at Parris Island. At that moment, and from the way I was being treated, I assumed that I was just going to be put out, and sent home, disgraced. When we returned from the PFT the senior drill instructor screamed my name, and the names of a few others. He ordered us to, "pack our trash" and report outside. I had no idea what was happening, and was even more nervous than ever before.

After I packed my things, and reported outside, a bus pulled up and we loaded up. After a short drive across the island, we ended up at the rifle range, which housed a physical conditioning platoon. This was a special place for recruits who could not meet the minimum physical requirements, but make no mistake about it, it was also a place that made you feel shame, and despair. I spent two weeks at the rifle range, and keep in mind, my training at this point had stopped all together. These days of torture were just bonus days at Parris Island. We worked out twice a day, and had all our meals monitored. After two weeks, I was able to run three miles, do fifteen pull ups, and eighty sit ups within acceptable times. It's amazing what two weeks can do for you under the right circumstances, and with the proper motivation. I watched as others quit, and I vividly remember feeling sorry for them, because I know they really wanted to make it. Of course, our own circumstances will dictate our ability or desire to accomplish things in life, and that is why we must be ready always to meet those challenges head on, dominate fear and overcome our own circumstances. Fear is a natural emotion, and the fight or flight response is real. Some people, when faced with fear, are laser focused on the situation, and they battle that which has created their fear. They overcome their fear with a great sense of faith, fury, and dedication to something greater. For these people, fear becomes something that propels them to reinvent themselves; fear becomes the motivator to never give up, and to always push forward. Then, you have those people who flee any situation that causes fear, to eliminate any discomfort or responsibility. Please don't misunderstand me, fear causes us to flee sometimes, and this does not necessarily make you any less of a person, but it does limit your ability to understand what you need to do on your journey leading others. At the end of the day, we cannot allow fear to own us, we need to own our fears, and make them work in our favor. Fear tempts us every day, and most of the time we don't recognize it as fear, we make sure that we don't call it fear because that would make us look weak. Never allow fear to determine the course of your life or leadership journey, and I promise you, the moment you start winning this battle you will be confronted with even more temptation to not act because of your fear.

    I was eventually returned to training, 1st Battalion, Bravo Company. My first day back was brutal because I did not know anyone, and the drill instructors had new recruits to break in. After returning to training, it did not take long to start fitting in with my fellow recruits, and I even think my senior drill instructor liked me for some reason. Of course, I was promoted and demoted numerous times, and thrashed on the quarter deck every night. One of the greatest leadership lessons I've learned was when I got fired as a squad leader.

    One day, our platoon was in the field, and our lunch arrived. Meals Ready to Eat, (MREs) are packets of processed food, and for the most part they tasted fine, but you had to be quick if you were going to find the food you liked. As a squad leader, I was responsible for collecting all MREs for my squad. So, I ran to the truck, collected all the MREs for my squad. Before allowing my squad to pick the MRE they wanted, I first took the one I wanted to make sure I had something good. One of my drill instructors observed me doing this. He ran over and got directly in my face, he was so close that his campaign cover was hitting me in the face.

He went off on me for what seemed like an eternity. He screamed in my face, "STEELE, WHAT DID I JUST FREAKING SEE? DID YOU TAKE A MEAL BEFORE YOUR TROOPS? WHAT IS FREAKING WRONG WITH YOU? DIDN'T ANYONE EVER TEACH YOU THAT A LEADER NEVER EATS FIRST? YOU ARE A FREAKING DISGRACE AS A SQUAD LEADER, GET THE FREAK OUT OF MY FACE…. YOU'RE FIRED. LEADERS ARE ALWAYS LAST, AND NEVER TAKE CREDIT FOR THE SUCCESS OF THEIR TEAM. LEADERS ONLY TAKE RESPONSIBILITY WHEN THEIR TEAM FAILS."

    Wow, fired and disgraced, but from that moment on I have never eaten first, and I've never taken credit for the success of any team that I've had the privilege to lead. The lesson was not about eating last, although if you get it, you understand the importance of this lesson. Over the years, I've been in numerous leadership roles, and none of them are different when it comes to leading others. Remember when I said, leadership is all about people, and how you lead them toward excellence in their world. I get opportunities to speak publicly, and at conferences all over the country, and I always eat last and give the credit for our success to my team of amazing educators. One day we were having a staff luncheon to celebrate the end of the school year, and the menu was amazing. After saying a few words, everyone got in line to make their plates, and start eating. After a few moments, I looked up and saw one of my assistant principals at the front of the line. Now, I did not treat him like my drill instructor treated me, but he and I have been talking about leadership for years now, and he knew better. Of course, I did not say anything to him, but after lunch, we were in my office just talking, and having fun, so I brought up that fact that he did not wait for his teachers and staff to go first. He said, "Man, I knew you were going to see that, but I was so hungry." We both started laughing, and I said, "Mr. Jones, our staff knows how important being a great leader means to you, and unfortunately, people wait to see us struggle with what we say we do, and how we live. Some people are waiting to see us fail. Being hungry and watching the food disappear before your eyes while so many pile food on their plate is what we do, but today someone told someone else that you went first, and you have to protect yourself from that."

Now, that may seem silly to some, but it really isn't. Every time we have a luncheon or dinner, someone always says, "Let the principal go first, or Dr. Steele, get you something to eat." I never go first, and never will. I will always consider everyone else in the room, before I consider myself. The truth is, most of the time the food is gone before I get a chance to go through the line. I've gotten use to fellowshipping with everyone, and then going to get something to eat afterwards, it's just a very small token of the sacrifice that is necessary to be a great leader, and trust me, too many great leaders sacrifice everything to serve and protect those they lead. Be great, selfless, and an inspiration for everyone you encounter. Don't miss those amazing opportunities to bring joy and inspiration to others.

So, when we returned from the field, my leadership lesson was not over. That evening, just before we were ready to turn in for the night, I heard my drill instructor scream, "STEELE, GET

YOUR ASS UP HERE." The quarter deck is an area outside the drill instructor's office, and any time they felt like it, which was often, they would call you up to the quarter deck and "thrash" you, which means make you do mountain climbers, push-ups, bends and thrust…. It was a place that helped you reflect on all your failures that day, or at least what you should be thinking about moving forward. I guess my drill instructor wanted to put an exclamation point on my earlier lesson, and he did. The harassment never stops while you are in basic training, and there is a very good and intentional reason for that. The military is charged with protecting this amazing country and all its citizens. To do that, we needed to learn, not only what it takes to protect this great country, but also what it means to follow orders. It seems today that many of our young people have not been taught how to respect others and follow orders.
Remember "A Few Good Men" when Jack Nicholson said, "Learn how to follow orders or people die." Well, that is fundamentally true. When you are in a life-threatening situation, it is crucial that you can follow your training, follow orders, and survive.

   The psychology of military training is so amazing to me, and I am so very thankful that I persevered for four years. Having someone tell you what to do, and following that order without question does not come easy to most people, and that is why most people do not join the military. I've had hundreds of people over the years tell me that they always wanted to join the military, but couldn't handle having someone telling them what to do all the time. I guess it isn't for everyone, but I'm so thankful I made that decision because it set me on a powerful journey. Following boot camp, I was sent to Oceanside, California for training. When I first arrived, I and one hundred other Marines were advised that our initial school had already started and that we were not going to be able to start for ten weeks. I had heard numerous stories about these types of situations, but I just hoped that they were not true, but here I was in the middle of one of those military stories, were they changed everything without your approval. I'll never forget Gunnery Sergeant Gonzalez coming into our barracks shouting, "Get dressed out, we're going on a run." Gunny Gonzalez was a very short and stocky Marine, and he could run for what seemed like forever. I thought when I graduated from boot camp I was in good shape, but after ten weeks with Gunny Gonzalez running ten miles was a daily occurrence, and although I hated it then, I learned to love running, and to be driven towards excellence. Sometimes, it's those things that we avoid or dread that shape us into the person we want to be. Embrace what you think you don't like, and attack those things that you dread. You will find character and courage in overcoming, and concurring things that you don't like or dread.

  Oceanside, California is on the coast, and the base, Camp Del Mar is on the beach. Every day, Gunny Gonzalez ran us several miles down the beach, and then up through the mountains. Although I learned to love it, and still do, I was not a fan at the time, because it was not what I signed up for. You see, most of our disappointments come from what we expected to happen or what we think should have happened. When we set ourselves up like this, we are certain to find great disappointment in this world. I'm so glad that I learned this lesson early on, and although I slip sometimes, and still get disappointed, I know that I am responsible for my success, my happiness, my attitude, so I need to make sure that I am in control of those things. Trust me, I did it, and so can you.

After my time in California, I was stationed with the Fourth Marine Division in New Orleans, Louisiana. While many of my friends were very disappointed because they were being sent to Japan, I was given New Orleans. I wanted to go to Japan, and I had many friends that wanted New Orleans, but for some reason it did not work out for everyone. I went to see my commanding officer to request Japan, but he denied my request, so it was off to the "Big Easy." This is just another example of how you get to choose your attitude toward life, and others. I'm certain that many of my fellow Marines used that decision to rationalize poor choices, and although I have not seen any of them since that day, I hope and pray they did not. I was not that disappointed because New Orleans is not that far from Tallahassee, Florida, where I grew up and all my family lived.

I settled in New Orleans rather quickly, making friends and getting involved in whatever I could. I worked out a lot, and played sports on my free time. I remember always being eager to learn and get involved in whatever I thought would be good for me, so when I was asked to join the color guard, I jumped at the chance, and am so thankful I did. In 1985, we were asked to present the colors before the Super Bowl. I got to see the 1985 Chicago Bears play from the sideline. Don't ever hesitate when something good comes your way, you never know how it will turn out. I think many people are fearful of stepping outside their comfort zone, and this prevents them from finding what is missing in their life. Life is about experience, and working toward a greater understanding of you, and what makes you unique.

I'm not trying to be philosophical, but think about it for a moment. We spend countless hours, even in our sleep thinking of ways to make us happier, or more satisfied with life. We think about how much money we have, or make, and how much we could make. We dread Monday, but praise Friday, and we are constantly planning things so we have something to look forward to. I'm sad for all those people who have already decided that Monday and Tuesday are days of despair, and that no joy or happiness can be found in them. Now, when Wednesday comes, people start thinking about the weekend, so much so that we have named Wednesday "hump day." If we can "get over the hump" then we can look forward to a few days off that will most certainly bring happiness and fulfillment to my life.

This is what I'm talking about friends. When you find the balance in your life that you are seeking, you will look forward to every day, and you will even be able to acknowledge and appreciate those days that don't go so well. I love rainy days. I love to sit outside under our back porch and watch and listen to the rain. I encourage my children to go out and play in the rain all the time, because rain does not mean you must sit inside, staring out the window wishing it wasn't raining. Of course, if it was lightening they had to come in, but Florida showers are very frequent, so playing in the rain was a wonderful thing growing up, and I wanted to teach my children to always find happiness in every circumstance. I want others to learn how to play in the rain, and stop staring out the window and thinking about how your life could be better, or how you could be happier. I want all of you to get up and create for yourself, and your family a life of excellence.

A few months into my new assignment, I overheard my commanding officer (CO) talking with our training captain about a school in California called Water Safety and Survival Instructor (WSSI). He was not happy because he had no WSSIs in his command, and the last two Marines he sent to California were not able to pass the course. I was nineteen-years-old, and I'll never forget, I walked into his office, and said, "Sir, I'm sorry for interrupting, but Sir, I can pass that course if you give me the opportunity." I worked in training, so the captain was my captain, and I think initially he was not happy that I interrupted, but would eventually be glad I did. The CO dismissed me without an answer, and only said, "Thank you, Marine." After the meeting with the CO, my captain said, "STEELE, GET IN MY OFFICE!" "Sir, yes sir," I replied as I walked in. He said, "Steele, do you have any idea what it takes to pass this school? Do you know what you are volunteering for? If I send you out there, and you fail, there will be hell to pay." I said, "Sir, I have no idea what it takes to pass this course, but I know you must be a strong swimmer, and I am. If you send me, I will die before I fail, sir." I had no idea what I was getting myself into; I just knew that the CO needed this, and that I would be in a select group of individuals who would have an opportunity to pass this course. I would later find out that this course is one of the most difficult courses in the military to pass. A few months later I arrived in Coronado California for WSSI School.

Every day for several weeks, we swam in the ocean, and training tank, which is military slang for swimming pool. We ran mile after mile, only to come back to the swimming tank to swim more miles. We mastered ten different swimming strokes, learned first aide, and how to teach others to survive in the water. I remember one of our rules, if you left any article of clothing or any materials behind after each day you would have to swim an additional one thousand meters, per article or book. After swimming and running several miles, the last thing you wanted to do was swim another one or two thousand meters after the day was done, but that is exactly what we did. The school was so difficult, and the retention rate is so low because most people can't deal with the mental aspects of drown proofing, or the underwater swim requirements. Most schools in the military are not that difficult to pass, and there are safe guards to ensure that you do pass. Some schools allow you to take the final test several times, and the instructors help you, but not WSSI. If you failed any test twice you were done.

I'll never forget our final test. Demonstrate mastery of all ten strokes, stay afloat with your hands and feet tied behind your back for thirty minutes, and then swim fifty meters. Finally, swim the length of an Olympic size pool underwater, with one breath. The underwater swim was what got most students. Some would make it with only ten feet to go, but would come up, they just couldn't overcome the mental aspect of holding their breath when you think you can't any longer, so they were sent home the day before graduation. They were not even allowed to stay one more day to watch graduation. I can't tell you the number of times I thought I was going to drown, or pass out from exhaustion. I can't remember how many students passed out, and had to be pulled from the water because they were drowning. You must know what it feels like to drown, especially if you are going to be responsible for teaching others to swim and survive in the water.

      I could not fail, because I made too many assurances that I would not fail, but most of all, I promised myself that I would not fail. This attitude has followed me till this very day. I'm certain I feel this way because of what I had to endure to get here, but honestly, I would have drowned before I gave up. As a leader, you will certainly have times where you think to yourself, is this all worth it. I can just give up, and things will be easier. I can make excuses or blame it on something else. Things are never easier when you quit. The difference between people who quit and those who don't is how they set themselves up to learn from failure or just fail. Some people have a tough time understanding that failure and uncertainty is a significant aspect of leadership, if you are continuing to learn and grow from it. I have numerous examples of people who wanted to quit, and could have, but refused. Never quit.

Me getting promoted to Corporal

That's me, first rifleman. I was so honored to serve with these amazing Marines and on this incredible color guard. 1985 Super Bowl, Bears v. Patriots. What an honor to be able to present "Old Glory" to such a large crowd. I love America!

Boot Camp photo, Private First Class Michael Steele, January 1984

This is me on the right attending my brother Bobby's graduation from Parris Island.

I am very proud to have served with my brother. OoRah and Semper Fi, my brother.

## Unselfish Love & Unwavering Character

When I first met my wife, Joyce, she worked out and took great care of herself, but was not a runner per se. She would hit the gym with me, by herself, and just get it done, and sometimes she would run, but I think she would say that she was not much of a runner. Several years later, my wife came to me and told me that she wanted to train for and run a marathon. She just wanted to do something that was going to be a challenge, and would honor my ex-wife, Marcia. You see, my ex-wife had cancer, and my wife and ex-wife had become close over the years, because my ex-wife and I had a beautiful child together, and wanted to make sure that our divorce never impacted her. My wife, is such an amazing and loving person, someone who loves all people, through all circumstances, no matter what. Most of all, my wife never quits. How many people do you know that hate their former spouses, with no consideration for the children involved? Better yet, how many wives do you know who want to sacrifice and honor their husband's ex-wife? I've seen divorce numerous times in my own life. I've seen firsthand what selfishness and ego do to children of divorce, and my ex-wife and I were not having it. So, my wife started training. For nearly one year she trained. Each week the miles increased until she was finally able to run 26.2 miles. She was so excited on the day of the race. She and her friends gathered, and got ready for the start. I remember being so proud of her, because usually she was following me around and supporting my races, so I was very excited to be able to support her. It was very warm that day in

Jacksonville, Florida, and the first four miles were on the beach. The race started, and there she went. Do you know what it's like to train so hard for something, and then accomplish it? How about going to school, when you feel like all the odds are against you, until the elation of graduation? It feels amazing to accomplish something that required pain, sacrifice, and courage. Several hours went by as we all waited at the finish line. Me, my ex-wife Marcia, and our amazing children waited, and waited. Most of the course was not assessable to viewers, so the start and finish lines were the only places you could really see the runners. We did not get concerned, but knew about what time she would finish the race, and when that time came and went we started looking down that long-hot road waiting to see my beautiful wife to appear. After what seemed like an eternity, there she was. She was running with an obvious limp, and from the look on her face, excruciating pain. Without hesitation, my ex-wife, ran on to the course and ran next to my wife for the last mile or so. She did not assist in any way because she wanted my wife to finish the race on her own. She wanted her to finish on her own determination. When she came across the finish line, she collapsed and had to be carried to the medical tent. We were all overwhelmed with emotion for her courage, grit, and unwillingness to not finish what she started; to never, ever quit. She made a commitment, and nothing was going to stop her from honoring that commitment.

  Life gives us choices every day, and we get to decide what choices we make. We get to determine how we will allow the pain of life to influence our decisions. Will we overcome it, conquer it, moving forward in a powerful and encouraging way, or will we quit. Will we allow the unforeseen or pain to keep us for honoring what we started? What is your pain, or disappointment threshold? At what level of pain and disappointment will it take for you to quit. Friends, can you see the power of this story, and ask yourself what is holding you back? What's holding you back? It really is easier than you might think. You want your marriage to be better, then work at it, and stop just hoping things will change. You want to be a better leader, then work at it, be intentional about what you want, and honest with who you are.

    A few years later my ex-wife Marcia came over to the house. She told me that her cancer had spread to her bones, and that she was going to be researching options, but it did not look promising. Through tears I told her that if she ever needed anything all she had to do was call, and she said, "Michael, I love my family and friends, but I know that if I ever needed anything I would call you and Joyce first. I'm so thankful for being a part of your family, and I truly feel like I am." You see, over the years, my wife and ex-wife had become close friends. No, it wasn't always easy, but when adults can learn how to communicate, and love, anything is possible. Our children called her Aunt Marcia, and they loved her very much. Marcia's cancer spread to her spine, causing her to be paralyzed from the waist down. Now you must know Marcia to appreciate her courage and never quit attitude.

    Marcia loved being fit, and she exercised tirelessly. She never left the house without being properly groomed and dressed in the latest and greatest fashion. When she was going through chemo therapy, and her hair started to fall out, she, like many just had her head shaved bald, and then went to purchase the most expensive wigs. Marcia was an amazing person, who loved having fun, and celebrating everyone. She just wanted to make sure that everyone was having fun, and enjoying life. Her attitude was contagious, and her love of life something to be admired.

  A few years later, when her cancer got to a point that doctors would no longer treat it, and Marcia was losing her battle, I was talking with my wife one night, and telling her that I was concerned about Marcia's final days. My wife said to me, "I'm going to call her and tell her to come live with us during this time." I was hoping she would say that, because I wanted the same thing. So, without hesitation, my wife arranged for a hospital bed to be placed in our home, and Marcia moved in. Being paralyzed and caring for someone in this condition was something that we were not ready for, but Joyce never showed any signs of regret, and she is a nurse so that was very helpful. My daughters and wife would help Marcia clean and take care of her personal needs. I would pick her up and carry her to the car every time we went to dinner or the movies, and every Saturday morning, I would make a Starbucks run for a skinny latte. Yes, even in her last days she wanted the "skinny." We all got into a routine, and we knew if she was with us she would be loved and cared for. I promise you, she was as much of a blessing to us, as we may have been to her. She never quit, and we all learned so much from her. Here is a woman who was in shape, was beautiful and loved life. Now, she finds herself paralyzed, with not much hope of living much longer, and she never quit. Her attitude was always positive, and she would even tell our children that they better not ever quit doing great things in this life. She went on and on with advice for our children, and to this day they still talk about her. One night we had to take Marcia to the emergency room because she was having difficulty. When she got checked in, a young handsome doctor walked in the room. Marcia, in pain and scared said, "Who is he, and is he married?" Her love of life, and her attitude was amazing. Even under these excruciating circumstances, she remained positive.

When she realized that her time was getting close, and I think she knew, she called a friend in Orlando, Florida and asked to move in with her. We insisted that she stay with us, but she would not hear of it. To this day, I'm convinced that she knew she was dying, and she did not want to burden us with that. She did not want us to see her die, so she moved to Florida. I only hope that I have that kind of courage and character when death is at my door. I only know that if you quit then you will never know how amazing your influence could be on others. In death, Marcia inspired me, my family and everyone she knew. She never quit, felt sorry for herself or complained. Marcia died on April 2, 2012.

What is holding you back? What keeps you from having the courage to never quit, and to lead with a compelling passion unlike anyone has ever seen. Great leaders do not quit. They learn from life's pain and disappointment, but never quit. They serve the needs of others, and do it with a profound sense of joy and pride, knowing that they are helping others overcome their own pain and disappointment. My Marine Corps days came and went very quickly, and I have so many stories, but I don't want this book to be five hundred pages, I just want it to encourage everyone to lead with passion, courage and a never surrender, never quit attitude. Well my time in the Corps was up, and after four years I was honorably discharged. I was not sure what I was going to do, but I knew I would serve my country or community in some capacity. I knew that helping others achieve and realize their potential was exactly what I wanted to do. I loved serving my country, and I still love and honor her to this day, and till the day I die. I learned so much about leadership and service in the Marines, and I am forever grateful for SSgt. Winchester, for his leadership, and example. OoRah SSgt. Winchester.

My wife and children in the medical tent following a grueling 26.2. My wife is so amazing. She trained and trained to complete this race. She suffered and overcame a lot to finished, but she never quit, and she did it all for Marcia, my ex-wife who was a part of our family. I am so proud of you Joyce…

My wife on the right, and my ex-wife in the back. Two amazingly beautiful women, incredible mothers, and more courageous then anyone I've ever known, especially after marrying me.

"Hope dominates fear every time. Be courageous and purposeful in your daily walk with others. Helping others find hope is your true calling. Never, ever quit."

– Dr. Mike Steele

## Still Searching for Purpose

After serving my four years in the Marine Corps I returned to Tallahassee, and took some time to decide what I wanted to do. Keep in mind, at the time I did not have any college, and I could not find work being a water survival instructor. A good friend of mine who served in the U.S. Army suggested I go to the Law Enforcement Academy with him. A few weeks later, I enrolled, and he and I attended the Lively Law Enforcement Academy in Quincy, Florida. The academy was somewhat like the military, a lot of orders, wearing uniforms, shooting, and physical fitness, but for me it was having a job that was challenging and respected. Once again, I was looking for that opportunity to distinguish myself, and felt that being a police officer would be awesome. The academy was an excellent experience, and I got to study and work along some outstanding men and women. I have several family members who have served or are still serving in law enforcement, and I'm very proud of that.

Following the academy, I was offered a job at Florida State University. At the time, Florida State had a small police force, but it was a great job, and first job I was offered. If you haven't realized it yet, I believe in loyalty, and I told myself that I would take the first job offered, so I did. You may think that working as a university police officer is easy, and that things don't happen on campus, but for those who know otherwise, please fill everyone else in. All types of crime happen on universities across this country, and my experience at Florida State was outstanding, not to mention I was a huge Florida State fan as well. Because we were small, not all of us got to ride in a patrol car, and since I was the rookie, I usually got assigned "foot patrol" which sounds bad, but is quite fun. I enjoyed walking the campus, meeting people from all walks of life, observing class, and all too often, walking up on people breaking the law. Foot patrol was old school, but a great lesson to start off my law enforcement career.

After a year at FSU, I applied with the Orange County Sheriff's Office in Orlando Florida. It took a few months, but I was eventually hired, and started with field training. Field training is a period where new deputies or officers go through to basically prove they can do the job. I would ride along with seasoned deputies for a two-week period, before starting another two weeks with a different Field Training Office. The entire field training lasts approximately thirteen weeks, if I remember correctly. I was eager to complete field training, and to finally get out on my own. Orlando is a wonderful place, and is considered the tourist capital of the world, but make no mistake about it, there is plenty of crime. When I finally completed field training, I was assigned to what then would probably be considered one of the busiest areas of town. This area was known for violence and drug use, and no matter what time of day, it was always very active. Back then I was so young and eager to prove myself, and so sure of myself that it didn't necessarily bode well for me all the time. Yes, I could find bad people, and catch them as well, if not better than most, and I rarely lost a foot pursuit, but I had so much more to learn about life, much less law enforcement. After working on the road for a year, I was selected to work in a uniform drug unit, which patrolled a very troubled neighborhood, well known for drug activity. My new supervisor was on the S.W.A.T. team, and I instantly became very interested in being a part of this very special group of law enforcement officers, so as soon as I was allowed, I tested, and joined the S.W.A.T. team. Sometimes, things can happen faster than they should, and being part of this elite unit may have been one of those times. I was young, and cocky. Looking back, I probably should have waited until I had more experience before joining such a team. It's hard to be patient when you want something so bad, especially if you think that it will bring more fulfillment or joy. Of course, I loved it. Shooting all day, flying around in helicopters, and building relationships with some of the best law enforcement officers anywhere. Honestly, I would have rather joined, and learned from my experience, instead of waiting. I think most people put off doing something they want because they are too afraid of making mistakes. Some leaders do this all too often, and they also do not encourage their followers to try new things, and learn from their mistakes.

One night I was coming home from a S.W.A.T. call out when I observed a suspect that we had been looking for in the car next to me. Of course, I was driving an unmarked car, so he did not recognize me as a law enforcement officer. I started calling for a marked patrol car to try and stop this individual, as I continued to follow, it didn't take long for this suspect to see that I was following, and he started fleeing. Eventually, I ended up chasing him on foot, and when I caught him there was a brief struggle. However, this all happened before my backup could arrive, and although I was kind of proud of myself for making this apprehension, a few others were not so happy, because I violated some policies and officer safety rules that I should not have.

    The following week I got called into my Major's office, and I'll never forget what he said. He said, "Steele, give me your badge and gun, you are suspended for two days. You need to learn now, early in your career that catching the bad guy is not the only thing that matters, people, and the community matter more. I will put you up against anyone with regards to apprehensions, but you must learn how to follow rules, and policies that are put in place to protect you and others. You endangered yourself, and potentially others by going off halfcocked. You have a brilliant future ahead, but you must learn this lesson." So, I left feeling somewhat dejected, but also empowered. I really appreciated how my Major explained the situation, while delivering a much-deserved dose of accountability. I learned a great deal from doing what I thought was right, but learning later that just because you think it is right, does not always mean it is good and blameless.

    Because there is always so much happening in big cities, you never knew what was going to happen next. One moment you are going to a simple theft case and the next a complex murder scene. One moment, you may be on your way to an alligator call, and the next, a disturbing child abuse case. It was non-stop, and at any moment your life could be changed by what you witnessed, or experienced. I think that law enforcement officers and military personnel have such an issue with post-traumatic stress disorder, because of the unknown, I know I certainly did. For some reason, going to a murder scene, or even a child abuse case did not have the impact on me mentally as it may have for others, but one day, unexpectedly, I got a call that would change my life, and career. And the leadership lesson I would learn from this call would force me on a journey of suffering, and uncertainty.

One day, I was working the day shift when I received a drowning call. It is not unusual to get drowning calls, because Orlando has so much water, and most people have pools in their back yards. Most of the time, by the time you arrive either the person is doing well, or the paramedics are already on the scene. On this day, I got the call, and I just happened to be in the area. As I arrived, I noticed that I was first on the scene. As I pulled up, an elderly man, carrying a young child was running towards my vehicle. It was obvious that he was scared, and the child was in serious distress. As soon as he could, he gave me the child, and I'll never forget the fear I saw in his eyes. The child was lifeless, and before I could start CPR, paramedics were on the scene. They literally grabbed her out of my arms and drove off, because they knew she was in serious trouble. I remember standing there in that front yard dazed at what I just experienced. I feel like it would have been better if I would have at least had a chance to help her, but the paramedics were quick. So, as you can imagine, I went through an unbelievable amount of emotions in a very short period, and I still had to investigate what happened to this child. Life happens so fast, and sometimes we are not prepared for it, and this was certainly one of those moments. I don't know if it was because I had a two-year-old daughter at home, and we had a pool, or if I was just overly vulnerable that day. What I can tell you is that the emotional response I experienced from this call was something I was not prepared for, and something that changed me forever.

      I requested permission to go to the hospital to follow up on her condition, and to make sure she was going to be fine, but was denied. OoRah Leadership accepts no excuses for not demonstrating genuine care and concern for everyone, especially those you lead. Leaders, future leaders, whatever you do, make certain that you demonstrate a genuine love and concern for those you lead. Never use excuses for why you did not demonstrate love and concern especially during tough times. Now, you aren't perfect, and there will be times when you fall short of your responsibility. Recognize those times and apologize to those impacted by your choices. You can do it privately or publicly, either way it is very powerful when those you lead see your humility. When you are in a leadership role, no matter if you are the boss, or a parent, or friend; you must take action that is intentional, purposeful, and meaningful. Here are a few things a leader could have done and made an incredible difference in my life, a difference that would have saved me from a great deal of heartache:

- A leader would have known me well enough to know that I was hurting.
- A leader would have considered my feelings, and potential traumatic stress that could have resulted.

- A leader would have immediately considered potential reactions and responses to my feelings, and my request to go to the hospital and check on this little girl. (I realize that some might be thinking of all sorts of excuses why the leader should not be responsible for all of this, but you would be wrong. Excuses are just that, excuses, and if you accepted the leadership role you are in, never use excuses. You will not always get it right, but never excuse yourself from not caring about those who follow your lead. Be intentional about caring for and praising those you lead. Let it be known that this is important to you, and that you will be consistent with it.)
- A leader would have cared enough to ensure I was going to be well. (Care about your employees, genuinely care about them. For many this is very uncomfortable, but absolutely necessary nonetheless. Learn how to care about your employees, and realize how powerful this is. This can be so much simpler than some make it. Ask your employees how they are feeling, and establish a safe and comfortable place where they feel safe talking to you. You must create this atmosphere where your people seek you out in times of need or in

times of mentoring. Don't be so caught up in you, or the bottom line that you allow an employee to miss out on your genuine care and concern.)

This is so simple, and for OoRah Leaders it would have gone much deeper. I realize we have a job to do, but I've said it before, and I'll keep saying it, "It's all about people. Your people are more important than anything else." I have over one hundred employees, and over eleven hundred students, so it would be impossible to impact them personally every day, but I try. What I can tell you, is if you have a desire to impact others, you can. So nearly every day I pull a staff member or student into my office and just praise them for something I've observed. I use the intercom to praise as well.

You see how simple that is? Leading others and genuinely caring about them is one of the greatest privileges you will ever have. OoRah Leadership demands that you, the leader, continue growing in your practice of leading with honor, integrity, and concern for those you lead. Don't be fooled by books, or speakers who tell you to embrace your specific leadership style. They are just trying to limit you, and your power to be excellent at all aspects of leadership. Don't let others tell you that you don't have to tell your spouse you love them, if you are demonstrating love in other ways. Don't listen to excuses about why it's hard for you to tell others how you feel, just conquer your fears, and make it a powerful part of who you are. Personally, I try every day to make sure that when I'm feeling it, I'm also sharing it as well. If I told my wife how much I loved her every time I thought about it, I would be doing it all day, so of course I'm not constantly texting or calling, but I'm open with her about that, and I share my complete thought about how that feels. Why do you, or we limit ourselves to how powerful we could be? What is it that prevents us from being that open and honest person we wished we could be? I don't want to keep beating a dead horse, but we have much to learn and plenty of room to grow in our OoRah Leadership practice. Be mindful, intentional, consistent, and excellent with those you lead. Honor them above all, and don't be afraid to let them know that you care for them.

    I worked in numerous capacities as a deputy sheriff, and enjoyed every assignment. I served as a Field Training Officer, Firearms Instructor, Critical Incident Stress Counselor, Auto Theft Detective, and School Resource Officer. I have way too many stories to tell, so I will be more to the point. In 1998 my wife and I sat down and talked about what we wanted for our family. At the time, we had three young children, and we were not very keen on staying in Orlando, so after my ten-year anniversary, we both resigned, and moved to Tallahassee Florida. I want to point out that our plan was to move, and we did so without jobs, and on faith. I can't begin to tell you how unbelievable it is to act on faith, and persevere through hardship. We eventually found jobs, and continued our journey in Tallahassee. Of course, I was very familiar with Tallahassee, having grown up there, and most of my family still lived there, so it was not an entirely crazy move. Ten years in law enforcement, especially in a city like Orlando will change you, if you let it. I'll never forget when I told my sister Carla that I was going to be working in law enforcement. She started crying, and said, "That job will change you, and you have such a big heart, I don't want that job to change that about you." Carla worked in law enforcement, and knew what I would be experiencing. She was worried it would change me, and in some ways, she was right, it did.

Me with two of my fellow Marines. When I worked in law enforcement, I had the honor of serving as a School Resource Officer, which is where I realized that I should change careers, and start helping children.

# Transform your School or Organization with OoRah Leadership

There was a time when Stratford High School in Nashville, Tennessee was one of the most sought-after schools in town. Stratford was a neighborhood school, and had a very proud past. To this day the alumni from Stratford are amazing, and supportive, but for a long time they were extremely disappointed in what had become of their treasured school.

In June of 2010, I was hired as the Executive Principal of Stratford High School. After my first interview, which was over the phone, I was asked to come to Nashville for a face-to-face. I was literally in my second interview for approximately 20 minutes when I was informed that I was hired, and that Stratford would be my school. Those in the room looked at each other, smirked, rolled their eyes, and one of the district administrators even said, "Congratulations, but don't forget your body armor." Sometimes people try to be funny, but really make themselves look rather stupid. No wonder the school was failing, if those who are supposed to care, don't.

Following my interview, I was introduced to my new supervisor. She too had nothing good to say about Stratford, and so I just tuned her off for the most part. Leadership accentuates the positive, and possibilities about what excellence looks like. True leadership acknowledges struggles, but will always immediately start considering what is going well, and how awesome things could be. As we continued to talk, my supervisor started sharing data with me. She mentioned that Stratford was considered one of the most dangerous schools in Tennessee, and that it was in the process of "state takeover" because the academic progress was so low. She went on to say that there were sixty-eight physical arrests out of Stratford the year prior to my arrival. I quickly realized that I was hired because of my background, and that I was expected to transform a troubled school.

Following our conversation, she handed me my keys, and told me to go introduce myself to my new secretary. No, she did not drive me to the school and introduce me herself, and there was no other introduction. From a leadership perspective, I am always baffled by the number of opportunities people miss. This would have been an amazing opportunity for my new supervisor to drive me to the school, show me around, and introduce me to as many employees as possible, but instead she chose to just hand me the keys. You see, you have opportunities every day to do amazing things for others, but all too often, we intentionally or unintentionally miss those opportunities. How often have you thought about telling someone you love them, but never do? How many times did you plan on speaking with your wife or husband, and just telling them how much you care about them, but for whatever reason, you don't. The same applies to your work environment, leaders. You have many ways to communicate with your students and employees, yet many leaders don't use them at all. We must not allow our egos to interfere with our ability to support, encourage and motivate those around us. Great leaders are constantly looking for ways to inspire those around them. So, my first impression of my new supervisor was less than stellar, but could have been amazing had she not wasted an opportunity. I can assure you, transforming Stratford High School had everything to do with taking every opportunity to encourage, support, defend and inspire our students and faculty.

Starting in the middle of the summer worked out well, because I got to meet a lot of people, and as I talk about how we transformed Stratford, and how you can transform your school, it will be very important to be specific on how to move forward. Everyone always wants to meet the new principal of the school. Some want to meet you because they are just curious. Some want to meet you to decide whether you are going to be a "push over", and then there are those who want to meet you because they want something from you. I can't tell you the number of businesses and churches who promised to do so much for the school, but never followed through, but I must say that there were also so many businesses and a few churches who have been outstanding.

After meeting so many students, parents, teachers, and community members, it didn't take long to figure out the main cause of the school's decline. When students and parents came to meet with me, they were just interested in what I was going to do to solve the school's problems. Parents were understandably concerned with the school's rapid decline, and students were equally concerned with their future in a school that had a reputation for being dangerous. I had already anticipated that only a few of the churches and businesses would follow through with their commitment because I've seen that before. However, I quickly realized that I had two types of staff members. First, I had those who wanted to be at Strafford, and wanted to do whatever it took to see the school grow into what it is today. These staff members, loved children from all walks of life, no matter what their ethnicity or past. These staff members were committed to do what was necessary to turn this school around.

Second, you have those who enjoyed working at this school because it was failing, and had a horrible reputation. You know the kind of employee I'm talking about, right? That employee who wants to do very little, and never be held accountable for results. I'm referring to employees who make excuses for why they are not successful, personally and professionally, and want to blame everyone or everything instead of owning their own incompetence. You see, there are those out there that have a job, but don't want to work. They exert energy finding ways of being lazy and unethical instead of just working hard and striving for excellence. Every organization and school have people like this, and the mission is, to either help them reinvent themselves or move them on and out of the environment you are trying to create. Excuses are just that, and leaders should never allow excuses to infiltrate their team.

I remember my first meeting with my new staff. There were about seventy-five staff members in the library, waiting for me to come in. I walked in, introduced myself and said, "We are a team from this point forward, and let me tell you team what I've discovered over the past month or so. It's not the students who are making this school horrible, it is the adults." Well, as you can imagine there was total silence in the room, but truer words had never been spoken. I mean at the time the school only had a 59% graduation rate, which is entirely unacceptable, and the adults were the reason for it. Discipline was off the charts with nearly forty-eight hundred referrals the previous year, and as I previously mentioned sixty-eight arrests. Now, I'm not talking about arrest made by our School Resource Officers, I'm talking about having to call 911 to get more police to come to the school and make physical arrests. Leaders and ethical adults do not allow this to happen in a school, and if you are currently in a school where you see these things happening on a regular basis, I can assure you that it starts with the leadership. It starts with you, principal.

Making excuses for why you are not successful or happy is very typical for most people. Many people do this, mostly because they don't understand any other way. Ask a teacher why her students didn't do better on the exam, and she'd say "because you or they don't do... It's because their parents don't care and support me. You don't understand what I have going on in my personal life." I've heard them all, and of course all these things are factors, but when you make them excuses they become permanent in your mind, and relieve you of all responsibility. When you allow excuses to filter into your life, office, or classroom then you have already given up on the excellence you hope to achieve. Personally, I don't accept excuses from my own children or my staff. I only accept ownership, and a plan of action to make it better. Don't come to my office and tell me that it's the parents fault, and that "these kids" can't do the work. As a matter of fact, I've told my staff that the term, "these kids" is no longer acceptable, because psychologically when one says, "these kids" they are taking their own ownership out of the scenario, lessoning their own responsibility. So, when one of my staff members

has a concern, I want to make sure I'm listening, and being supportive, but they must say, "my students" because then it becomes personal, and is easier to take full responsibility for you own actions.

You see, you can make excuses about what you have going on as much as you want, but at the end of the day, you will not grow unless you take ownership of your own problems. I can assure you that if you are going through a struggle right now, at this very moment, you are part of your own problem. You see you get to decide every day how you are going to respond to disappointments in your own life. You get to choose how you will treat others, and how you will lift others up, or bring them down. Your problems are yours, and although it is always a great idea to find help and support, you must acknowledge that what you are experiencing, and what is making you unhappy or unsuccessful, is your problem. It's not because you don't make enough money, or that someone did this or that. It's not because your wife or husband won't do this or that, and it is certainly not because your students won't be perfect, that you are feeling this way.

So, as you can imagine, my first staff meeting was very short. After explaining to my staff why we were to blame for the current condition and status of the school, I then explained my expectations moving forward. I then asked all the athletic coaches to stay behind for a short meeting to follow. I went on to explain that we were going to turn Stratford into a science, technology, engineering and math (STEM) school. I'll never forget one of my assistant principals who was an African American man saying to me in an open meeting, "These kids can't do this work." Remember, we were serving a school which at the time had a population of 90% African American children. I paused before replying to his poorly thought out comment, and when I did reply, I said, "That is exactly why this school is where it is. We have teachers and leaders in this building who will tell others that all children can learn, but don't really believe it themselves. We are going to be a STEM school, and these children will do great if we are great. You all need to decide if you want to be great, because if you don't, we need to talk."

    Leaders, why wouldn't you want to be great, especially when you've been given such an amazing opportunity to lead others? Do you remember the story I told you about the drill instructor chewing me out because I was eating before my men? I have never forgotten that lesson, and to this day will never eat a meal before my team does. Leadership takes courage, and hard work, and I can assure you that if you are experiencing success otherwise, it is a fluke that will soon come back to punish you. How could this administrator have made such a statement in front of all those people, and how in the world could he believes that just because the majority of students were African American, they could not learn? If members of the administration felt that way, how easy would it be for the entire staff to feel that way? We, the adults are responsible for what happens in our schools, and the truth of the matter is, some adults have no business working with children, if they are only going to celebrate those who are easy to work with. So, it is not too difficult to see what I was working with from the beginning, and the changes that needed to be made if we were going to have the impact we wanted, and anticipated.

    I discussed things like character, and integrity. I told each staff member that winning was not my priority if we had to cheat or behave unethically to do so. I was adamant that I did not want a single victory if it meant we were being unethical in the process. This meant also allowing athletes to play that were ineligible, failing a class or had issues with discipline. In Tennessee if a student has a 2.0 GPA the semester prior, then they are eligible the next semester. I was not good with that, and implemented a policy that if a student was failing any course, they cannot play in any competition. No, they were not kicked off the team. As a matter of fact, I wanted them to remain on the team, just not play in the games until they were passing every class. We all know that it only takes a little work to earn a "C", and that was the new expectation, that they were passing every class.

    Several years ago, I worked in a private K-12 school in Florida. I served as an assistant principal and athletic director. One day after football practice, the starting quarterback, running back and center decided to urinate in another young man's locker, and all over his belongings. I suspended each young man for several days, which included the day of our next home football game. My principal at the time, who I consider to be one of the finest men I have ever known, was so strong under pressure from parents to allow these young men to play in a silly middle-school football game. I'll never forget one parent, who came to meet with us. His son was one of the better players on the team, and was being suspended. As we sat in the meeting, he insisted that his son get to play, and I was so proud of my boss for making it my decision, and if you know me, there was no way these young men were going to play in this game. This is amazing, and when I think about leadership, this is one of those moments that come to mind. My principal was speaking with the parent about his son's veracity, and the parent said, "I don't know why you are making such a big deal about him lying, it wasn't even a big lie, and it's ok to lie occasionally, right?" I remember it like it was yesterday. My principal looked at me, grinned, and then looked at the parent and said, "No, it is never ok to lie, and I can't believe you are sitting here asking me to be ok with the fact that your son lied continuously about his involvement. What he and the others did was wrong on many levels, and I support Dr. Steele's decision." Parents don't usually defend their children for the sake of the children, they defend them for their own sake. You see, it makes no difference how big your house is, or how much money you have, you can almost always look at the parenting when you see a child doing such despicable things. I've known hundreds of parents who tried so hard to give their children everything, except what they needed most, discipline. Most parents don't even consider discipline a form of love, because having to discipline their children requires courage, courage to know that it will be uncomfortable for you when you discipline you children, and it will also hurt. Yes, we still won the game, but not by much.

After the game, a parent, who had remained silent through the entire week came up to me and said, "I want to thank you for what you did, it took a lot of guts, but the rest of us saw it, and our children saw it. Thank you." You don't always have to be vindicated when you stand your ground, and do what is necessary, but it sure feels great to know that most people care about character, and they want their children to grow up with discipline, and integrity. Transforming a troubled school is not at all an easy process, and there are numerous moving parts that must be considered. Consider the following when you start on this mission.

## The Mission

Mission statements are different than vision statements. A school or organization of excellence needs to have both. In your mission statement, only talk about what your mission is. I know the new trend is to be short and sweet, but I want to encourage you to let your entire team work on the mission statement, before deciding. When you have decided then make it public, and refer to it often. This is our mission, and we will always be on mission. I have our mission statement throughout the entire school and we discuss it, and are reminded of it often. Don't allow your mission statement just to be something that everyone is doing. Make it meaningful and purposeful from the start, and hold the entire team, especially yourself to it every day, and don't be afraid to change your mission parameters as needed. Your mission statement let's everyone know what you stand for, and what your goals are for your school or organization.

## Vision

Do others know what your vision for your business or school is? Does the team know where you are trying to go? If not, then there needs to be a more direct intentionality for your vision. A vision statement talks about where you want and hope to be in the future. Again, your vision statement can be short and concise, but don't hinder yourself or what could be just to make it short. Create, and then share your vision with your team. Be inspired and motivational when you share it. Have your team so excited to be a part of something special.

### The Outstanding Guidance Counselor

Every school, especially those schools who expect to be highly successful need guidance counselors who are not only exceptional, but who also understand how important their role is. All too often you see guidance counselors being utilized in ways that were not designed for their level of education and expertise. Guidance counselors must have a master's degree to be licensed, as well as a practicum. This level of education should allow others to assume that guidance counselors not only wanted, but completely understand their role. There is no way our school could have been as successful as we have without our amazing counselors. I would put our counselors up against any in the country with regards to knowledge, work ethic, and team spirit. My counselors are "get the job done" kind of people. Follow these simple rules if you want to maximize your counselor's expertise, and accentuate their positives:

- Allow all your counselors to serve on your administrative team. Counselors often feel caught in the middle of being a teacher or being

an administrator, so while they are more than willing to serve as teachers, make it very clear that they are welcome on the administrative team, and include them in the decision making of the school.
- Find a department chair or team leader. Make sure this person wants the position, and understands the responsibility for the position. Also, make sure this individual is rewarded for their willingness to take on a leadership role, which is so important to the overall success of the school. Be very clear with this new leader what your expectations will be, and hold them accountable.
- Allow your counselors to be counselors, and not glorified clerks or test examiners. All too often counselors are asked to do things such as proctor exams, and prepare schedules. Yes, this may be a function of their role, but should not dominate their day. Call counselors in on discipline, and other student's needs that you become aware of. Have your counselors prepare professional development for the

staff, or do guidance lessons for students.
- At the very beginning of the year, audit the counseling department. Do so with the intent of making sure there are no major issues before starting the year. Have your counseling team do audits for each nine weeks or per semester, whichever is more feasible for you, but make sure that records have no discrepancies moving forward. Again, this is not just an accountability tool, it helps the entire school run smoothly.
- Ensure that all student contact is documented. This is an area that you do not want to miss. In an uncertain world, children have proven time and time again that they can and will make poor choices. You always want to make sure that every counseling session is documented, especially if a child is talking about hurting themselves or others. You can never get in trouble for documenting, but you always open yourself up when you decide not to.

## The Exceptional Teacher

Many school districts tell principals how to interview prospective teachers, and in many cases, make them ask the same questions, so there is little autonomy, creativity or instinct involved. My assistant principals make fun of me because when I interview teachers, I rarely ask them about their classroom management or instructional strategies, I usually leave that up to my assistants. I do this because, although I want my teachers to be great instructors, I care more about their ability to be part of a team, to be loyal, and to be dedicated. I can teach teachers how to be better behavior management experts, and I can help them improve on their instruction, but I want people working for me who know how important it is to serve on a team, a team that expects others to take ownership of what they have been blessed with, and succeed. I want teachers who understand loyalty. Loyalty to me, their peers and our school. Loyalty is the most important characteristic a teacher can have. I would much rather have an average teacher, who has an amazing attitude for life, learning, and love of others, than an amazing teacher who has a bad attitude. We can teach everything else, but without these qualities you are taking unnecessary risks. So, what does the exceptional teacher look like?

The exceptional teacher is first and foremost someone who loves life, and has happiness and peace in their own personal life. All too often when a teacher is not performing well or responding positively to constructive criticism it is because they are living a life of uncertainty. A life where they can't seem to find happiness, and peace, so it naturally comes to work with them, and makes it difficult for them to understand why what they are doing is so important, especially to our students. Over the years I've met numerous teachers who were not only great people, but had unlimited potential if they could figure out a way to not allow their own personal issues to impact their jobs. Divorce, illness, financial problems are just a few stressors that impact the lives of not only teachers, but all professionals. Unfortunately, teachers do not have the luxury of coming to work and not engaging their students and co-workers. So, when facing personal problems, teachers, often must put them aside while they are at work, and the only thing that is going to help them is to create an environment where they feel safe, comfortable, and supported.

    A few years ago, I interviewed a teacher candidate, who also wanted to coach football. I had already received a few references that were not stellar, but I believe in giving everyone an opportunity to reinvent themselves, so I called him in for an interview. During his interview, we talked openly about his past experiences, and some of the struggles he had in his previous positions. He assured me that it was mostly not him, but others who misunderstood him. I informed him that his explanation sounded a lot like excuses, and we all know that excuses are unacceptable. I offered him the position, even though a few others warned me not too. I think part of me wanted to show others that he could be successful in the environment that we had created at Stratford.

School started, and it did not take long for me to start receiving complaints about the very things I was warned about. Some said he had a harsh tone, not with the students, but with his colleagues. Others said, he was intimidating, and unfriendly, so I called a meeting and spoke with my new teacher. From the onset, he started making excuses and defending his actions. He was posturing his position to protect himself from, not only responsibility, but future accountability. Think about that for a moment, because many of us do it. Think about the number of times you anticipate a response or outcome, so you posture to make yourself less vulnerable. What I recognized was happening with this teacher and coach was that he had been posturing for so long it became his "go to" defense mechanism. So, I changed my dialogue and mannerisms from that of accountability, to a supportive role.

I said to him, "Coach, you are safe here. You don't have to worry about me or anyone else not supporting you, or having your back. You don't have to worry about your job and future here if you are willing to be on this journey with all of us. I'm not going to just expect excellence out of you without the highest level of support." At first, he was very uncomfortable with this strategic conversation, and I suspect that no one has ever said these things to him. He started to respond with some typical manly response, and I said, "Coach, you are safe here, and you can be everything you've wanted to be." At that very moment, this very large, former college football player started sobbing. It took him several minutes to collect himself, and it was truly amazing to see years of stress and fear fall off his shoulders to the floor. It was unbelievable to see the look of security and prosperity return to his face. At that very moment, he knew that he no longer needed to walk around the school with a chip on his shoulder, protecting himself from an invisible fear. Since that moment, this outstanding teacher and football coach has been amazing. He smiles, laughs, cuts up with me, and does an awesome job with our students. I am more than proud to have him working with us, and had someone only seen his pain and potential years before, they would have had an excellent teacher and football coach, but more importantly, an outstanding person on their staff.

- The exceptional teacher is highly motivated to see others succeed. He/she is always prepared and excited about what they can possibly teach others daily.
- The exceptional teacher fears for his/her student. They fear that they may fail to teach them the essentials

for prosperity and hope for their future.
- The exceptional teacher is highly ethical, making sure no one ever has reason to question their character or integrity.
- The exceptional teacher lives their life in a way that inspires others to seek what they have, and to emulate their love of life and education.
- The exceptional teacher is loyal, loyal to themselves, their students, peers, and school. Loyalty is essential for the truly exceptional educator, and without loyalty there will be no true success.

Principals, and leaders, you must be willing to expose yourself, and have these types of interactions with your staff. Every job in the world, especially in education is about the people, not the numbers. Great leaders not only know how to inspire, but they can't wait to inspire others. I'm certain we've seen individuals in positions of authority, and yet they have no interest in people, no passion for others, and although they may be experiencing a certain level of success, I can assure you that they have not tapped into the unbelievable power of inspiring others to excel.

## The Courageous Leader

If you walk into a book store you will easily find an entire row of books dedicated to leadership. You will see books on assorted styles, philosophies, and they come in all shapes in sizes. My recommendation for you is to not identify yourself with one specific style of leadership, and embrace all aspects of leadership. Identifying with one specific style hinders you and your willingness to be courageous. Over the years I've heard so many people say, "I am a transformational leader" or a "transactional leader." What are those, and what do they mean? OoRah Leadership demands excellence at all times, and does not identify with a style of leadership. True leadership is about having others who want to follow you and your vision for numerous reasons.

First, and foremost, followers want to follow you because they believe in you, and the only way to get them to be loyal to you is to demonstrate that you genuinely care about them. Leadership styles don't really exist. Great leaders don't choose a style, and then abandoned aspects of other approaches. Awesome leaders can be successful in all walks of life, and in all circumstances.

During my first few months at Stratford High School, I spent a lot of time evaluating programs and people. I don't believe in letting people go for no reason, and in some respect, if I let you go then I too have failed to live up to my ability to develop and lead you. I truly believe that everyone has the ability to be outstanding, and if given the opportunity and support can excel. Unfortunately, not everyone is outstanding, and they don't want to grow towards excellence.

As I evaluated my new staff, and various programs in the school, I came across a very interesting young man, Mr. Vincent Jones. My first encounter with Vincent was in our first coaches meeting, where I asked him and the others to resign. Of course, there was not a lot of getting to know each other in that meeting, and I'm certain that when it was over, Vincent really did not care for me too much. Leaders must always remember that those you lead or serve deserve for you to always have their best interest at heart. Did I want to fire all my coaches, no, of course not? Did they however need to know that I was serious about being ethical in our practices, yes, absolutely?

At the time Vincent was an unlicensed special education teacher and football coach. His main responsibility was to teach or babysit our students with the most behavioral issues. These are the most difficult students in the school with regards to impulse control, anger and discipline. Vincent, and his assistant did a great job with these children with respect to keeping them out of trouble, but they were not being educated to my satisfaction. I had walked around and considered Vincent's room numerous times. Every time I looked in his window or walked in, Vincent and his assistant were sitting behind the desk talking, and the students were either talking or doing some type of work sheet. In times past this was considered, "doing an excellent job" if these students were under control, but after every visit I became more and more infuriated that the two adults in the room were demonstrating a lack of care or knowledge for what these students would endure if they did not graduate from high school, and develop the skills necessary to succeed. I would later find out that Vincent cared very much, and was very knowledgeable, he just simply had no one show him what caring, and leadership can actually do for children.

I methodically waited, and then requested a meeting with Vincent and his assistant. Until this point, both had avoided contact with me, I guess hoping I would not notice their lack of excellence and desire to be outstanding. As they entered my office, I noticed how close they were, they were good friends, and I also noticed that they had become dependent on each other, to rationalize their lack of desire, motivation and understanding of what excellence looks like. Remember, I demand excellence in all things, and at all times, and so should you, not only in your personal life, but in your professional life as well. When you work, and especially when you work with children there should be no question that you are living a life of integrity, and that you bring that to work with you every day.

It's important to note too that Vincent is also an African American man, and the relevance of this will become clearer shortly. It is also important for readers to know that Vincent has given me his blessing to write this piece on courageous leadership, using his miraculous example.

Vincent was a very large man, obese, and if you were observant you could easily tell that he was uncomfortable, and lacked confidence. His size and lack of self-esteem were keeping him from what I know he wanted, which was a life of excellence, and not just at work, but at home as well. You see, I also noticed from the very beginning that Vincent was not only very smart, articulate and passionate; he also had a pure heart. He wanted those things in life that make us unique, joyful, and proud, but for reasons I would not yet know, he did not know how to go about achieving these things. I started our meeting by asking Vincent what was going on in his classroom. He thought about it for a few moments and started off with the same dribble you might expect, but he knew I was not buying it. I told him that during every visit all I noticed was him sitting behind the desk talking with his assistant. I'll never forget what he said to me. He said, "Sir, I, we watch the toughest kids in the school and they stay out of trouble when they are in my room." I believe this is the most significant problem with struggling teachers; they have no vision for what could be for every student. If you can lead, inspire and show teachers how to care for every single child, then you will have a game changer on your hands, but for those teachers who just can't seem to find that in their hearts, they should reflect very seriously about their future in education.

  I did not argue with him or have any type of smart response; I simply told Vincent that what he was doing as the teacher of record in his class was unacceptable, and I wanted it changed. I further explained that my expectation was that he was to challenge his students to not only behave, but to learn as well, to be pushed to excel. I expected him to confront his students and himself with obtaining excellence every day, and in all walks of life. He knew, and I could tell by the look in his eyes, I was right, and that he had simply been 'existing' for years, babysitting and coaching football. He knew he had to change, and I could tell that he wanted to change. What he struggled with at the time was having a white man care enough about him to even mention these things. You see, this meeting was not about how unsuccessful you are, rather how successful you could be. I told him that I cared about him and his future, and that I wanted him to be great in all aspects of life. I'll never forget how he sat there and listened to everything I had to say, soaking each and every word up. He never uttered a sound until I was done talking, and then when I was done, he said, "Yes, sir." Little did he or I know that our first meeting, no matter how pointed it was would lead to not only an amazing friendship, but a mentorship unlike no other.

      Leaders, you must take time for people, all people. You walk into the Wal-Mart and not just say hello to the greeter, but give that person some time. That greeter is most likely an elderly person who needs that job to pay for medicine, and it only takes a moment to say hello or shake their hand. It only takes a second to call the restaurant manager over to tell them how great someone is doing. Be intentional about how you are with others, especially those close to you, and when you must admonish someone, do it with restoration in mind, not power or control. Always make sure that you have a plan to restore others so that on their journey they grow, and appreciate you for helping them. Never be afraid to talk with people in good faith. Good faith simply means that if you care for someone, then you should not worry about being open and honest with them. In Vincent's case, I had not yet mentioned his weight or lack of motivation, but if I truly cared for him, and truly desired to see him succeed, there would come a point that I would have to speak with him about those things that were keeping him from the joy and success he so desired, that we all so desire. If you are fortunate enough to lead others, and are unwilling or unable to have very difficult conversations with them, I promise you that you are not being as effective and successful as you could be, and you are certainly not demonstrating the care and concern for others that should be evident.

Following our first meeting, Vincent and I met frequently on and off for the next month or so. He no longer avoided me in the halls, and would come around my office more and just talk. In other words, I really started to like Vincent, and I believe he started to trust me a little more as well. One day, Vincent and I were sitting in my office, and I said, "Vincent, are we friends?" He replied, "I think so, why do you ask?" I said, "Vincent, I care about you, and your family. I want you to know that I have no other intent but to see you be successful and happy, and I know that you don't feel either right now." He replied, "Well, you know I just do my job and go home. What else is there?" At that very moment I was not going to let anything get in the way of mentoring Vincent Jones. I told Vincent that I was his friend, and that if he was able to handle me being his boss and friend then I was good with it. I further explained that if he wanted to go down this mentoring/friendship road that he would have to be able to deal with the fact that as his boss I expected excellence in all things, and no excuses for failure. After he acknowledged in the affirmative, I said, "Vincent, what are you doing with your life? You have six beautiful children, and their mother is amazing, but you have yet to marry her. You are in your thirties and your weight and health won't have you around to see your children graduate. When are you going to start taking care of yourself, and make your family legit? What will it take for you to change the things that are keeping you down?"

    Yes, that is exactly what I said give or take a few words here or there. My question was, where all his friends and other mentors had been throughout the course of his life. How is it that no one else had the courage to speak with Vincent in this manner, and to care enough to try and help him. Courage, and courage under fire is a core leadership trait for those who want to experience leadership at a level unlike no other. Yes, I took a small risk that Vincent would be offended, but I was willing to take that risk because I cared that much about him. I've had numerous conversations like that over the years with family and employees who, just for whatever reason, can't see themselves being happy and successful. Do you remember when I talked about the two essential questions of who am I, and who do I want to be? Vincent had no idea who he was, and if he did, was ashamed to admit it at the time. He knew he wanted more, and was wasting time, but he did not have clarity on who he wanted to be. Over the course of several months Vincent and I talked, fellowshipped and built a trusting relationship that transcended employer and employee. It's ok to be friends with your staff, if everyone understands and respects boundaries. Vincent changed his life in every way imaginable. He not only sees his future as bright, he understands what it means to seek excellence in everything he does.

Vincent does an amazing job keeping me from getting a sideline penalty. I am more than proud of the journey Vincent started many years ago. OoRah, Dr. Vincent Jones.

### Creating Identity

When you create the person you want to be, and identify with who you want to be, then you can start to achieve those things in life that will truly transform you. Transforming Stratford was no different. We had to identify who we were, and when we did that, the overall picture was not good, not good at all, but we had to be honest with who we were as a school and staff. Yes, there were already great people working at the school, but there were way too many who had no idea what leadership, integrity and sacrifice meant. So, when we started to have transparent conversations about who we were, and who we wanted to be. Now we could start forming our strategic plan to change, and acknowledge that change, and transformation would not come without hard word and sacrifice.

      Creating your own identity or creating an identity for your school does not guarantee success over night, but it does start you on a journey that will not only transform your school, but yourself as well. And, by creating this identity, and making sure that everyone knows your vision, you will attract those who want to live a life of purpose and meaning. It will be so much easier to recruit and retain highly capable individuals who want to work in the environment you have created.

      It did not take long, a month or so to have some real conversations as a staff about who we wanted to be as a school. I challenged the staff however with also deciding who they wanted to be as individuals. What kind of husband, wife, brother, sister, son, daughter do you want to be? Have you lived up to the potential that you have within you? These are questions that we all should be constantly asking ourselves. In May 2017, I meet with my staff just before the last day of school. I met with them to apologize to them because for a few months I was off mission allowing other things to infiltrate my mind, and character. No, it was nothing immoral, but for me it made no difference because I was letting others down, and that is not something I'm comfortable with. I stood in front of one hundred or more people and said, "I want to apologize to each of you, and tell you all how sorry I am for being off mission these past few months." Someone immediately said something like, "It's cool Dr. Steele we know how busy you are and how much you support us." Although I was thankful for that, I really needed my staff to hear me, because as I've already said, being intentional and not missing opportunities is vital to your leadership success. I said, "Thank you, but please hear me out. I appreciate you all having my back, I really do, but I allowed myself to be distracted, and I should have recognized it before a few days ago. I want each of you to know that I am reinventing myself as I encourage you all to do. Next year, I am going to act like it is my first year at Stratford and we are all going to do remarkable things." Being vulnerable is not a terrible thing for leaders, and honestly it can be a very powerful thing if it is genuine and sincere, and I was. Of course, my staff is amazing, and they had my back, and it felt amazing. Leaders should never have a problem apologizing when they are wrong, but unfortunately you don't see it very often.

  Have a great conversation with yourself, and then pull in others as needed, but discover who you are, and be honest with yourself. If you are the kind of husband who is not constantly focusing on his wife and family, then own that and change. It's not impossible, and a fantastic journey if you have the character to see it through. Identify who you want to be, and then create a plan of action that will help you achieve your goals.

  What ever happened to Vincent? Well, friends, Vincent finally did what it took to get his teaching license, went back to school and received his administrative license a year later. One day he came into my office and told me that he was interested in an administrative position at a nearby middle school, and asked me if I would call and give him a good recommendation. I told him to sit down, and I called the principal on the spot. The following morning, after his interview, Vincent was offered the position as an assistant principal. For three years Vincent used OoRah Leadership to help transform that middle school. In that time, I did not see Vincent that much, but learned that I would have an assistant principal opening the following year, so I called Vincent to check his interest. To my satisfaction, he was very interested in returning to Stratford where he started, and he has been working here ever since. Vincent is more than ready for his own school, has completed his doctorate degree, and now has others asking him to mentor them. Oh yeah, I forgot to tell you, Vincent has lost over one hundred and forty pounds, works out every day, and is driven to be excellent. Yes, he finally made the mother of his children his wife. His family is amazing, and I could not be prouder of him.

    Remember when I mentioned that Vincent was African American, and that I am white? Vincent once told me that he has never really had any white friends, and that growing up near Atlanta, had no white friends. I never gave it much thought, but in our conversations Vincent would tell me about others who warned him or made fun of him for having a white mentor. When Vincent would speak with his father about his new boss, and how he was helping, his father had no idea that I was white, and when he found out was surprised, not at all disappointed, just surprised.

    Friends, we get in the way of our own happiness and success all the time. When you believe in your heart that love conquers all, and you live your life in such a way, then helping others transform their life and change their future is possible, but one thing is true, if you don't have a love for others, then you will never reach your leadership potential. Start creating the identity of who you are, and be vocal about who you want to be. Remember, missed opportunities are all on you, and it takes courage to be intentional when it comes to helping others.

# Inspire Excellence

## Amazing Support Staff

Way too often support staff feel like they are not valued, and thus not part of the overall team. I want to say up front that I have an amazing support staff of secretaries, custodians, cooks, and clerks. Each one is amazing in their own way, and they are all a significant part of our success. You must make sure that you include your support staff in all aspects of the school, and be intentional about designing missions that they can carry out and oversee.

The front desk receptionist is a key person in your organization, because she/he is the first voice or face visitors see. They represent the entire school or business, so it only makes sense to make sure you have an absolute gem in that position. When I first started at Stratford, my receptionist had a chip on her shoulders so big I was not sure I was going to be able to remove it. She was helpful, but she always seemed angry and unhappy. Remember the conversation I had with Dr. Jones, well, I had to have the same type of conversation with my receptionist. I told her that I valued her and cared about her future, but she would have to improve to keep her position. I explained that I needed someone that parents and students looked forward to seeing, someone who was happy, and eager to help. After a little banter, I asked my receptionist if she planned on answering the phone for the next forty years. She said, "No, but what other options do I have?" I encouraged her to go back to school, get her degree and open other doors of possibility. Then came the excuses, I don't have the time or the money. All my classes are in the day time, so I would not be able to work. After hearing most of her excuses, I asked her to close the door, and for the next hour or so, we talked about possibilities. I told her that I would allow her to leave work to attend classes, and would have one of our financial aid counselors speak with her about tuition. Over the past two years, my young attitudinal receptionist finished her AA degree, and got promoted to be my secretary and bookkeeper. She just recently passed the bookkeeper exam and will serve in that capacity next year.

It would have been too easy to replace her or transfer her, but we must slow down and be in a constant state of reflection that we are working with amazing people, and they are not expendable. Make sure you are giving everyone on your staff the time they deserve, and the mentoring and support they need. Have an open door policy, and stand by it. My door is open 99.9% of the time, and I am intentional about that, because I never know when a student, parent or staff member is going to need me, so when someone looks in my office, I stop everything I'm doing to address their need. This is the job, and to be highly successful, you must always focus on people. Get to know your staff, all your staff. Tell them how much you appreciate them, and honor them by being public with your praise and private with your admonishments. I can guarantee you, your support staff are every bit as responsible for your success as the rest of the team.

Finally, be intentional about praising these outstanding people. Make time to honor them, and reward their efforts, because they deserve it.

## Success with Minority Students

When I first applied to work in Nashville, Tennessee, I applied at a predominately African American school on the Eastside of town. I made it all the way through the process, and was going to be offered the Executive Principal position the following day. I wanted that job, and waited eagerly for the call. I finally got the call, but it was not good news. I was advised that the community heard that I was going to be offered the position, but they did not want a white male at a school serving mostly African American students. I was then offered another school and asked to come to Nashville for a face-to-face interview.

During that meeting, I was told that the school I was being considered for was already offered to someone else. Ironically, during that interview I was offered Stratford which at the time was serving 90% African American students. If you haven't learned that ethnicity is not at all a factor in the potential success of others, then you have much to learn my friends. Over the past seven years at Stratford I have been asked or questioned numerous times about finding success with young black students, yet I am white. That is true; I am a white male, in a predominately African American school. How could I ever be successful, being so different from most of my students? That is such a laughable thought, and believe me when I say, the transformation of Stratford is nothing short of a miracle, and all it took was love, discipline, sacrifice, accountability and more love. There is not a school in America that couldn't transform with the right leadership, and loving adults in place. And when I say, "loving adults" I mean the kind of adults who love children so much, that they don't tolerate any misbehavior from them at all. I'm talking about adults who will lower the boom and drop the hammer on students every time they deserve it, and then be purposeful about restoring their spirit, and building their dreams and hopes. I'm talking about adults who don't make excuses for themselves, and certainly don't allow their students to use them. You do this day-in day-out and you watch how fast your school will transform. The prevailing issue is that the majority of school leaders don't know how to love their students while also holding them accountable.

    Many of our school leaders are so uncomfortable showing appreciation for their staff, and celebrating their success. Great school leaders need to learn how do both, if they hope to lead a successful school, especially a low-income school. But let's be real, working with impoverished minority students is not easy, and that describes a large percentage of schools across this country. I wrote this book to be transparent about how anyone can change their life, find success, and transform a school or organization. So, being honest about how to best work with a challenging population of students is essential moving forward, but it is nearly impossible if you are not willing to have a different and unique mindset.

    According to the Center for Disease Control (CDC) 70% of young black men who do not graduate from high school will likely end up in prison…70%. Now, I'm not aware of a more reliable source than the CDC, but if this is even remotely true, then there should be an outcry so loud, and it should come from every living citizen of this country, as well as other countries. Remember when I first talked about Stratford's graduation rate, when it was 59%? I don't have the exact numbers, but if this is true, a lot of young black men went to prison because we failed to provide them with opportunities to graduate from high school. Yes, we failed, it is mostly our fault that this is occurring across our nation. If we keep blaming parents, and poverty then the pipeline to prison will never change. We are responsible for creating an educational environment where all students can succeed. We talk about differentiated learning, and how important it is, but I don't think we are even coming close to understanding what that means for impoverished minority students. No, I do not accept excuses from any of my students, and if they are black and poor, that means they just need to acknowledge their circumstance and decide to work harder. I'm very hard on my students, but I love them with so much passion that if they graduate from this school hating me, but having what it takes, that is a sacrifice I am willing to make. I think everyone will agree when I say that all students should be treated equally, fairly, and with compassion, but that is not happening, and if your graduation rate is in the high 50s or low 60s, then your students are not being treated equally, fairly, or with compassion.

I just made some readers angry, while others are saying, "That's right." If I made you angry, good. Don't be angry at me, or the truth. When I started at Stratford, and learned of our dismal graduation rate, I examined every transcript in the entire school. Yes, this required me to take work home, and stay late, but you have no other choice. Sacrifice is essential for all leaders. Although I did not do any data analysis, it did not take a genius to see that the number of seniors that were not going to graduate because they received a 68 or 69 in the ninth grade or a 65 in the tenth grade was astronomical. I would venture to say that at least 50% of my seniors had to make up work from previous years or they would not graduate, and yet we sit there and just expect them to do it. Come graduation day, if they did not make up their work, oh well, good luck to you.

As I write this, it makes me angry all over again, because those few points that prevented the credit doesn't mean that the student must do a little work to earn one point, they must do a lot of work, and in some districts, repeat the entire course to earn credit. Now factor in poverty, and all that comes with poverty, and tell me that we are treating our students fairly, equally, and with compassion. We all know that graduating from high school is a new beginning, a fresh start, and so many never had that because of a few points.... disgraceful.

Leaders, teachers, don't get in the way of those you are teaching or leading. You don't have to give anyone anything, and yes, I believe that everyone should work and earn their success, but do some critical thinking from now on, and demonstrate a better understanding of why you feel the way you do, and how others could benefit holistically from your new mindset.

    Not too long, after I started at Stratford, it dawned on me, and I'm ashamed to say that it took me so long, but it dawned on me that just because I was not prejudice, and just because I didn't mistreat those who were different than me, does not mean that I am part of the solution to help those who suffer such disparity every day. Yes, inaction equals no action, which also equals irresponsibility, and an uncaring heart. Trust me, the injustices that we see in our schools does not have to come in the form of blatant abuse, it can come in many forms, such as disparities in discipline, grades, state-wide testing, and graduation qualifications. Neglect and mistreatment can come in the form of not being intentional about saying "hello", or "have a nice day", or "get to class, now", or "I'm suspending you from school because you can't behave that way. I care about you, and I want you to succeed, but you need to understand…" Can you see what I'm getting at? We need to always slow down, and be intentional about our relationships with everyone, especially our students. I know, we all get too much fluff from our districts, but they have responsibilities also. Stop making excuses, and get this work done.

    One day I had to expel a young African American male student. He was constantly in trouble, and on this occasion had a zero-tolerance violation that mandated his expulsion. This young man was like many others, no father in his life, and a mother who had long given up on him, and was non-existent in his life. Like most young black men, this young man had great potential, but would he ever find hope? Explaining to this young man that he was going to be expelled was different than any other time I had to discipline him. He remained calm, and I'll never forget the look on his face of despair, and uncertainty. He left my office without any hostility or having to get the last word, which again, was very unlike him. The following day, I entered the school through the cafeteria. As I was coming out, this young man was walking in. I said, "What are you doing here, you are expelled. You are not supposed to be here, and could be arrested for trespassing." He said, "Dr. Steele, I've been looking for you. Can I please at least take my final exams because I know that I will not do well in the alternative school?" I don't know why, and can't explain the moment, but at that very moment my heart was broken. My heart was broken not only for this young man, but for every child that has no hope for their future.

    What are we doing, I thought to myself? How can we continue to allow so many young people to be thrown away essentially to end up in poverty, and susceptible to violence and sadness their entire life? After taking this young man to the front office and allowing him to complete his final exams, he left, and I've not seen him since. I returned to my office, closed the door and cried. No, I didn't just have tears in my eyes, I wept, and my life was forever changed, and my mission also changed. At that very moment I knew that I would never allow conformity, hate, or politics to get in the way of what I knew was right for children, especially our young black men, and although I never thought I did, I was confronted with what I hadn't done to help. The psychology of racism, or not liking or hating someone else because of the color of their skin is not as simple as others just being different than you. Over the years I have learned that people were trained either consciously or unconsciously to hate or devalue others because they are different. Fear, ignorance and self-preservation are just a few reasons why others devalue African Americans boys in our country and around the world. Fear is the most powerful and unconscious reason why so many hate and devalue our African American children, and I'm not just talking about white people. African American children are devalued by all ethnicities, including other African Americans, and for African American boys, it is much worse. It is as if our young African American boys have no chance unless they overcome so much, and it is not fair.

Just look up murder suspects, murder victims, highest dropout rate, and suicide rate. Our young black men are leading in every category, so you would have a hard time convincing me this disparity is not unfair, especially since our young black men equal about twelve percent of the entire population. I am so hard on all my students, especially my young black men. I'll never stop being hard on them, and loving them enough to be consistent every day. I love them, I love all my students, and in OoRah Leadership, there is no place for anything else. Never set aside how you believe, embrace it, and then change it if necessary. Never mask your prejudice, but change it because you have changed, and because you want to be excellent, you want to be an OoRah Leader. Can you for just a second imagine a teacher or leader going to their school or business and having a genuine dislike for a certain population, whether it is African Americans, homosexuals or white people? Can you just sit back and imagine how their lives must be when no one is around? It saddens me to think about these people, knowing the joy that they are missing by not embracing everyone. OoRah!!!

As a child growing up I remember not having much, and enduring numerous obstacles to survive. I recall times when my parents were gone for days at a time and my sister, who was not much older than me was forced to take care of her three younger siblings. Needless to say, it was not the best upbringing, but there was also much to be thankful for. As a child I don't remember ever being taught to be prejudice or to dislike others because they were different than me. I remember visiting my grandfather and hearing him use racial slur after racial slur. He hated African Americans with such a passion, and of course other ethnicities were not too far from his wrath either. I recall sitting there and having to endure his language because I was doing what I was told to do. It wasn't until years later that it dawned on me that many children are raised to hate others because they are different, and that fear and control that I talk about is instilled at an early age.

We are never going to change everyone. There will always be people who hate you because of your skin color, it is simply a fact. I don't know why we are not more intelligent as a society, but we are just not. Sometimes you can just see someone walking down the road, and the first impression is to not trust them, like them, or shy away from them, we all do it. OoRah Leadership demands that when you are feeling this way, you ask yourself why, and even speak with your mentor about your true feelings. If you want to change, you can, but there is no chance of success without being honest with yourself.

Several years ago, a good friend came to me for some advice. He told me a story about how his son was not doing well in school, and was getting in trouble more often than usual. He went on and on with the small stuff, and I knew there was more to it, but he was not giving it up. You see, parents are also in a protective mode when it comes to their children, and even though they know they have not been the best parent, and their child is absolutely wrong, they will still protect them, because that is all they have sometimes. I told my friend that he was wasting his time. He looked at me with confusion and disappointment. He said, "Why, what do you mean?" I told him he would never find a solution or have peace about his son's journey, if he could not be honest about it. He went on to tell me that his son had been arrested a few weeks prior for possession of marijuana, and that he was hanging out with the wrong crowd. He begged me not to tell anyone that he came to me, and even asked me to keep it from my wife. You see, that is the problem. When most people have a problem, of course they don't want anyone else to know, they want everyone else to think their life is perfect, and no cause for concern. This is an understandable feeling, but the exact opposite of what you should do. You can't go around telling everyone that "it takes a village to raise a child," then keep your child's problems a secret. Yes, I know it's hard, and embarrassing, but if you want to help, you will involve others, and in some cases, families are in such desperation, they have no other choice but to get everyone involved. I told you, this OoRah Leadership journey would not be easy. I told you, you will be confronted with what you need to change, not what needs to change around you. You must want this, and you can have it, you just need to change the way you think, and the way you have been taught for years.

So, what happened to me that made me realize that we, all of us, need to take a much closer look at the hope and future of our young black men? I can't be certain, but I remember seeing no hope in this young man's face, and I recall thinking that I will in some way be responsible for his future sorrow. I immediately had a feeling of regret that it took me forty-nine years to really see the disparity young black men in this world face. I can't explain what happened at that moment or why this young man was the one who caused me to feel this way, I can just tell you that it happened, and I'm better because of it. Do you remember when I said that I was not prejudice and that I was never taught to be that way? It dawned on me at that very moment that without knowing, I was behaving worse than someone who outwardly hates others. I was part of a system that did not truly embrace all children no matter what their background or ethnicity, and I was ashamed of myself. Yes, it is uncomfortable telling this story, but that is exactly what I'm encouraging you to do. I could omit this story, and be more comfortable that so many people never learned of my shame, but my shame is what inspired this book, and I'm elated that I was able to learn from it. Never be afraid to learn from your mistakes, the unintentional, and the intentional.

After a few moments I collected myself, and called a meeting with my administrative team. I shared my experience with them in detail. I truly believe they were all uncomfortable in the beginning because, for the most part, they had never seen me that vulnerable, but I could tell that they knew I was serious. I advised my team that we would be taking a different approach with our students, especially our African American male students. The first thing I did was rescind the expulsion for this young man and get him back in school. Yes, it was a zero-tolerance incident, but I made several phone calls until I finally got the answer and support I was looking for. You see, you don't ever give up when you are doing what is right and blameless for others. Think about that word, "Blameless", think about how powerful and meaningful that word is. Are you living a blameless life, a life that if others could see would be a life of love and integrity? Blameless, means simply that you cannot be blamed or responsible for failure because you have done and are doing everything you can to succeed, not only with yourself, but with others as well. You make sure you go the distance to ensure you are helping create hope where none exists.

My team already knew that I was an ethical person, and that I demanded integrity always, but I think for a minute they were taken back, because they already assumed we were doing everything we could for our students. When I explained further, they realized that we could be doing a much better job, and that there was no better time than now to start. I left work that day so energized and excited about this new mission. I couldn't wait to tell my family and friends, that out of defeat, there is victory. I had no idea that I would meet so much resistance on this new journey, but I would. This is exactly why we should all be in a constant state of growing and learning, because we are never going to have all the answers, but we can walk our daily walk with the assurance that what we are trying to accomplish, and how we are trying to help is blameless.

A few days after my epiphany, and by coincidence, I was speaking with a good friend. Now, my friend was about twenty years older than me, and he was African American. He had become my friend over the past few months, and in some ways, a mentor. I was so excited to tell him about my new outlook, and how I could not wait to share with others the importance of my new mission. He was such a great listener, and just sat there with a smile on his face, and listened while I talked on and on. Now, keep in mind, he is 70 years old, and has experienced an incredible journey. When I paused in my conversation he said, "Mike, do you want to know what has baffled me over the years? People keep saying that they love all children. How can they possibly love all children and see so many who can't read, or will never graduate from high school? How can they say they love all children, and continue to ignore the disparity for so many? If they truly loved all children, this wouldn't happen." Like me, he was very transparent. He always made sure that when he said something, there was complete clarity in what he was saying, and he made sure you understood him. I don't believe he meant that we don't love our children if some don't succeed, I think what he was trying to say is, stop using that term so loosely, because if we truly loved all children, we would be much more intentional and responsible for their success. If we truly loved all children, we would do more to demonstrate our love.

I explained to my friend that I had already created a presentation, and had been invited to speak at a very large conference in Nashville. He explained that he was excited for me, and that this message needed to come from a "white man." He said, "This message needs to come from a white male because black folks have been sharing this message of hope and disparity for years, but no one wants to hear from another black person about how difficult life can be for black people. This message needs to come from someone who has seen it, but has never lived it." Again, I was blown away by his comments, but had complete understanding and clarity in what he was saying. Yes, he was right, this message needs to be delivered by someone who has no other reason to share it, except the fact that there needed to be a change, for so many young people. He then said something to me that I will never forget. Not only will I never forget it, but it drives me to continue this mission every day. My friend said, "Mike, I think what you are doing is great, but I want you to know that if you do this, it will not come without potential hardship and sacrifice for you personally, and professionally. If you do this, you will offend many people, people who you know and don't know. You will offend people of power and authority, and will never know it. I want you to remember one thing, Jesus Christ was crucified for trying to spread love and hope to a lost world, and you aren't Jesus for sure, but you understand what I'm trying to say, right?"

I was immediately confronted with his comment, and said, "Are you serious? Are you telling me that others would attack me personally and professionally if I started down this road? Are you telling me that the hate is so powerful for some that they would try to hurt my career?" He said, "Yes, you will not come out of this without having offended some, and having others hate you for it." I immediately told him that I was not backing down from what I knew was right, and that if he was correct, then I was going to have to deal with whatever came my way. You see, I was glad that he said these things, and I know he was only trying to inform me, rather than stop me. I know he was just making sure I was aware of all the possibilities, but nothing was going to stop me from doing what was necessary for my students.

Isn't that the problem with so many leaders, their unwillingness to do what is right and blameless, instead of worrying about how it will impact their own life? Doing what is right, especially for those who can't defend or protect themselves is essential to what you should be wanting to accomplish for your school, students, and customers. Leaders, and future principals, when you decide to work in a school, any school, you are going to experience times when your character and integrity are being challenged. There will come a time when you will have to make a choice of what is right or what is best for you, and when you make the right call, which should rarely be what is best for you, you need to understand that you will most likely and without intent, offend others. When you are working in a school where your students not only need you to defend them, but would not succeed unless you defend them, you must realize that your life is going to change. Don't be discouraged, never be discouraged. Your work with students that don't have much, and have little chance of hope without a lot of love will bless your life in ways you can't imagine.

      I have a policy at my school that no student can participate in any extra-curricular activity if they are failing any class. Now, this policy is different from the policy that the Tennessee Secondary School Athletic Association requires, and is much more stringent. Students can still be on the team, and participate in practice, but they can't play. I want them to practice and realize how hard it is without the reward of playing, because they need to know how this world works, and you can't fail in life and be rewarded. You see, when we allow our children to be rewarded after giving no effort we betray them and set them up for heartache and failure. I don't take any excuses from my staff or students. I don't care what color your skin is, your orientation, or religious beliefs. I don't care if you are poor or rich, you must give effort to succeed. Just last week we cancelled a volleyball game because we did not have enough players to field a team, and I'm concerned that we will have many starters out for our football game tonight because they are failing a class.

      If you are reading this and thinking that it is too harsh, don't fool yourself. We are in a battle for these young people's lives, and I will not allow me or my staff to betray them to win a few games. For those of you who know me, you know how competitive I am. I want to win at everything, and I love all our programs, but I will not sacrifice a young person's future to win a game. You see it way too often, and I refuse to be a part of something that will ultimately hurt children. By the way, I didn't say that my students had to make "As" or "Bs", I simply said they had to be passing their classes. They must show effort, and desire to do what is good for them.

 Recently I was playing golf with a new friend. We were talking, and he was asking some great questions in an effort to get to know me better. He asked me what I thought my peers thought of me. I said, "I think my peers believe I am a man of character and integrity, and I think they trust me as a colleague. I've never given, and will never give them a reason to question my integrity, and they have all been able to evaluate my work for eight years now." He said, "That is almost verbatim what a few of your peers told me last week, but another told me that you tend to piss people off." I started laughing out loud, because that is the story of my life. I have never been one to not speak up when I observed an injustice, or felt that others were being wronged, so I said, "I'm certain that I've angered some people, but when you are the leader of a school that always has to defend your students, and your success, you are going to anger some people." He agreed, and we moved on to another topic, but I didn't want to move on, because a lot could be learned from this conversation. You see, when this mostly African American school raised our graduation rate, and started competing with other schools, we were questioned by some, even publicly. When our ACT scores started going up drastically, we were questioned about how, even publicly. When our discipline declined drastically, our data, and data entry were questioned, even publicly, and every time I defended my team, my students, and this community, but do you remember what my good friend warned me about? He is so smart, and he was right, we were challenged often about our success, and if no one will say it, I will, it's because we serve so many impoverished African American students.

I trust by now you are shaking your fist in the air, and screaming, "OoRah!!!" A little anger is a good thing, it makes you more focused and intentional, but I don't want anger to be your fuel, I want OoRah Leadership and action to be your fuel. Please allow me to offer to you some OoRah Leadership suggestions about having an impact on all your students, but especially those who suffer the most disparity, our young black men:

- First and foremost, decide in your own heart that you want to be a champion for your students, all your students, but don't be afraid to recognize that the disparity for minority students is real, and for young-black men, over the top. Keep in mind that young-black men are not just the highest in terms of drop-out rates, but they are also number one in murder victims, murder suspects, and now suicide rate. You must be honest with yourself, and your new mission. Let me stop you here, if you are not able or willing to go on this OoRah Leadership mission, then don't pretend. I'm talking about a mission unlike no other, and one that will

change your life and the lives of so many forever.
- Meet with your staff, and share your new mindset, and yes, change of heart with them. Speak with them openly about your feelings, and what the new landscape is going to look like in your school. Form a committee of volunteers, who want to develop a new outlook for your minority students, and how the entire staff could help impact their lives. Be excited about it, and never shy away from speaking out about it publicly. Remember, you are doing something that is blameless.
- Have your new mission and policies available for your staff during professional development, and before students return. Take all the time needed to make sure everyone understands what is expected, and what you hope the outcome will produce. You already know that you will have some that never think anything will work. Encourage them and try to get them on mission, but if they continue down that negative road, encourage them to find another mission, at another school. There is no place for negativity in this work.
- When students return, have class level meetings, and share not only your new mission, but share your own heart for the mission. Our

children are much smarter than we give them credit for sometimes, and I can promise you, they can handle this, and they will respect you for it, but it must be genuine, or they will not respond. At the beginning of every year, I meet with each grade level, and I speak with them about what they are facing if they don't graduate from high school, and I encourage them to love one another, and their teachers. I have open conversations with them about how hard it is to protect them and their school, but what an honor it is to do it. I speak with them like I'm speaking to my own children, and I treat them like I treat my own children, because in many ways, they are. Like you, I've purchased many lunches, shoes, clothes, prom dresses, and tuxedos. Like you, I've bought groceries and paid the rent, so in many ways, they are my own children, and I'm thankful for that. I will also meet with just the boys, and then the girls, and we will talk openly about various issues, and how we all can work toward a having a great school.

I remember meeting with my seniors one year, we were all talking, and they were all doing great. A young man said something about not being treated fairly after an incident, and although I was not the administrator that resolved that issue, I was aware of the circumstances. After he was done with his comment and question, I said, "How have you made our school better in four years, and how have you made my job easier? I went on to explain to the entire class some very specific things we do to protect them, and make sure they have the support necessary to succeed. He was very perplexed by my question, because he had never been forced to consider others, and only thought about himself. If we can get our students to start thinking in terms of serving and supporting others, then we will see a significant difference in behavior and excellence.

- Develop a core group of students that you will meet with on a regular basis, to discuss your vision for how to improve all circumstances for minority students. Allow this group to grow as large as possible, but have students come to you, and hold them accountable to take action and leadership in the school. Of course, you will have some that mess up, and you will put them out of the group, but always give them an opportunity to return. When a child makes a mistake, there is never a time where that child is "cut off"

from reinventing themselves...never. I try to remind myself very often that I was not the best student in the world, and many adults had to put up with me as part of their job. As often as possible, I try to consider that when I work with young people, and when I'm working with young-black men, I always make sure I am mindful to remember that the odds are stacked against them.
- Expose your students to positive messaging in the school. Yes, this should be common sense, but always be looking to evolve to the next level. Positive posters, quotes, handouts, you name it...do it. You can never have enough positive messaging in your building, and when you visit classrooms, make sure teachers have supportive and positive messaging in their rooms. I guarantee you, I can go to any school in this country and find students, teachers, parents or businesses that will not only help, but pay for murals, or positive quotes on the walls, you just must want to see your culture change bad enough, and then get it done...no excuses.
- Hold yourself, your staff, and especially your students accountable. Be open and honest with your students about your

expectations, and you must share expectations as often as possible. Remember, we are working with children, and even if they do hear what you are saying, they don't usually register it in their brain until they've heard it numerous times. Communicating your expectation is something that should be on-going, so much so that your staff and students will start making fun of you, or repeat what you say. The same is true with your message of love and hope. It's no different than your own children. Your students spend more time with you, than they do with their own parents, so why shouldn't they know how you feel about them. If this is a problem for you, then remember what I said…it's your problem. Your staff and your students should not have to navigate around your personal shortcomings, especially if you are not willing to continue growing in your OoRah Leadership practice. Let me give you an example of thinking totally outside the box, and always looking for ways to evolve. If we have a student who continues to stack up discipline referrals, we hold that student accountable, of course. When it gets to the point that the student is going to be suspended for several days, we give him/her a choice. The student can take the suspension, or they can call their parent/guardian and tell them that if they will come up to the school and have lunch with me and one of my staff members, then they would not be suspended. I do this because obviously suspending and expelling children rarely works. Yes, I realize that it is necessary sometimes, but it rarely works out for the child. I want to make sure we are always evolving to help people. Now, I know some of you are saying, "There is no way I'm buying lunch for this person or that person." If that is your mindset, then you are not being intentional about helping others, and your ego is interfering with your happiness and success. I don't care what you do, as long as it is ethical, but if you want to see true transformation in children who have next to nothing, you are going to have to put away the conventional ideas, and start making it personal. The best example, I can give you is giving a child a hug. Most people, who have no idea what they are talking about will tell you, you should not hug your students, or have physical contact with your students. This is "hog wash", and inspired by people who have been hurt, or do not know any better. Yes, it angers me when I hear of a teacher or principal violating the trust of their students, and abusing their authority to hurt a child, but those individuals are only far and few between. Children, your students need physical contact from time-to-time. Like you, I've had students walk up to me and just hug me, or ask for a hug. If your character is where it should be, this will never be a problem, and if you are living a blameless life, this will never be a problem. This only becomes a problem when you character and integrity are in question. If you are concerned about giving a student a hug, then call someone into your office like I do to witness the hug. I know some of you are thinking about what I'm saying and smiling because you give hugs, or high fives all the time. Never forget, we are working with children, and children need at least six positive interactions for every negative interaction, so when you correct a student, be ready, and willing to then give that same student incredible positive feedback when deserved. Look for reasons to praise that child often.

"Excellence is beautiful and, like all beautiful things, temporary. One moment we are victorious. The next moment we were victorious. An excuse, however, endures. An excuse promises permanence. Excellence is difficult. An excuse is seductive. It promises to end hardship, failure, and embarrassment. Excellence requires pain. An excuse promises that you'll be pain-free."

– Eric Greitens

## The Exceptional Principal

What does it take to be an exceptional principal, and do you have what it takes? I can assure you, if you want to be an excellent principal, you will need more than just the minimum educational requirements, and license from whatever state you work in. I've been fortunate to work with amazing principals over the past ten years, and I am very thankful for their example and friendship. Someone recently asked me what my colleagues thought about me. I thought it was a great question, and one that we should constantly be asking each other if we hope to continue our journey as exceptional principals. Notice, I used the word "exceptional." Exceptional encompasses outstanding, awesome, amazing, fantastic, and excellent. Exceptional means that you have mastered at a high level all aspects of leadership to inspire change when needed, motivate others always, admit when you are wrong, love and support those who follow, as well as those you serve. Allow me to share with you from my perspective what an exceptional principal looks like:

**Integrity Driven:** An exceptional principal is driven by doing what is right at all times. Their integrity must never be in question, and when it is, and it will be, especially if you are finding success in a school that serves mostly impoverished minority students, you should and must have all the evidence to support you, and your staff. I've had several people, privately and publicly question our graduation rate increase. Some people just don't believe that our staff and students were capable of such hard work and success. I've had people question our ACT scores, and the amount of scholarship money our students receive. They are not questioning these things out of concern; they are questioning these things out of ignorance. Without integrity you will fail. You may succeed in your own mind for a while, but you will ultimately fail, and in doing so, fail everyone who was counting on you. Let me detail how we increased our graduation rate, so you will see how it can be done. Do you remember what our graduation rate was when we started this transformational journey….59%? Unbelievable, and totally unacceptable. The first thing I did was to put on notice every employee that we would no longer accept excuses for failure. I then audited my guidance department and found guidance counselors who love children, weren't lazy, and had the work ethic and integrity to get this machine moving in the right direction. This takes work, but it is not that difficult. I promise you, if you need to and want to raise your graduation rate, this works.

1. First, and always foremost, never jeopardize your integrity. Be vocal at every meeting that unethical behavior and taking short cuts will not be tolerated. Make sure this message is heard by all.
2. Develop a "graduation cohort" team, which can include anyone in the building. Serving on our team I have all administrators, counselors, academy coach, deans of students, credit recovery teacher, my secretary, and anyone else wanting to serve in this capacity.

3. Develop your mission objectives, which are mainly to increase the number of students who graduate, keeping in mind the statistics I shared with you early about our young black men. Make sure the team knows that this is not voluntary, and each member needs to understand the amount of effort that is going to be required to see young people graduate from high school...no excuses.
4. Do not wait for your district to give you your graduation cohort list. Get your list as soon as school starts or earlier if possible. When I first started at Stratford, it would take months to get our list, and I never understood why it was so difficult, so I called the state department of education myself and got the list within thirty minutes. Do not wait for others to do the work that you can do yourself. Get your list and get started.
5. Assign an equal number of students to each member of your newly formed team, making sure they are aware that they are responsible for these student's success. Make sure you are fair, and not giving some team members students who all require a great amount of work. Yes, the principal also gets his/her list, and is equally responsible.
6. Have your guidance counselors color code the list, green = on track to graduation, yellow = has a good chance to graduate, red = needs a lot of work to graduate, blue = students who no longer attend our school, but are still on our cohort list and

will count against us if not located, and documented, white = special education students who will not earn a regular education diploma, and will subsequently count against our graduation rate. Yes, in most states, if a student receives special educational services, and is not capable of earning a "regular educational" diploma, they will count against your graduation rate. I have fought this all the way to Washington, D.C., and don't understand why I can't get people to listen. Treating these students in this manner is discriminatory, and unfair, but the reality is, you need to be aware of these students, because there are options to help them earn a different type of diploma that will not count against your graduation rate.

7. Have a senior meeting, and get contracts from each one indicating their willingness and desire to graduate. Talk with them about how they can recover credits if needed, and assure them that you are all there to help them succeed. Don't hesitate to share alarming statistics, and paint a picture of life without a high school diploma. Get their attention, and never forget that you must reach them, each of them if they are going to have a chance of hope. Keep the contracts in guidance, and make sure you have them until graduation is over.

8. Give your team a solid month to meet with each student on their own personal list before calling another cohort meeting. Your next meeting should happen in

September or early October. In your second meeting discuss every student who is at risk of not making it. That means every student that is not in the "green" category. Everyone on the team needs to know what these students need to graduate, and what they are working on. Of course, you don't have to just help your list of students; we can all help every student.
9. Make one person responsible for the cohort list received by the state. Remember, you can only go by the list the state has provided, but you must be thorough because mistakes happen at all levels, and students get added or dropped, and that ultimately impacts your graduation rate. As children complete work, or fail to do their work, indicate that on the color-coded list you have created.
10. Continue bi-weekly meetings until January. In January, start meeting once per week updating your graduation list as you go. Make sure your spreadsheet has enough room to annotate each student's level of performance, effort and feedback. Ultimately, if a student fails to graduate you want as much documentation as possible to show, whoever wants to see your data that you did everything you possibly could to see that student graduate from high school.
11. Develop a plan of action for summer school. If you don't have funding, find volunteers. If you can't find volunteers, then create opportunities using all twelve-month employees. The principal can supervise credit recovery if necessary. You

should have a good idea of what your graduation rate is going to be long before the state department puts out a final percentage, but you must create an atmosphere where hard word is expected, and excuses are not tolerated.
12. Principals, make sure you have documentation before changing grades, but do not be afraid to change a grade for students that have been working very hard to earn credit.

**Fair, ethical & consistent:** If you are already living a life of integrity then being fair, ethical & consistent should come easy to you, but you need to know from the get go that everyone is watching. People want to see that you are who you say you are, and I can promise you that if you are not, others will find out, and it will not only damage your reputation, but hurt your chances of being successful. Being fair and ethical means always considering what is not only right, but fair for all involved. To do this, you are going to have to listen, and understand all the information that will be brought to you. If a student deserves a punishment, then give them their punishment, no matter how harsh it is, but be willing to talk with them about your rationale. Explain to them why you feel they are deserving of such a punishment, and even ask them to offer a different form of punishment, but be fair and consistent always. We all want to support our teachers, but if the teacher is wrong then address it and make sure that she/he understands your perspective and why you are making the decision you are making, but be consistent, and fair. Before I inform my staff of a new mission, I make it very clear that we are not going to take shortcuts, and that everything we do will be highly ethical always. It is important that your message also matches your behavior. Do the right thing, and make sure others know you are doing the right thing.

Not too long ago I was given a reprimand because I had some audit findings. I can assure you that we can account for every nickel we are blessed to have, but I did break some rules, I guess. In the span of two weeks we lost two students and had another lose their house to a fire. My amazing students came to me and asked if they could raise money to help their peers, and of course I agreed. We organized a fund raiser, and were able to give each family approximately $500 a piece, but I guess these types of fund raisers violated some rule, hence the reprimand. This is a perfect example of how we, the adults get in the way of doing what is right. Somewhere, someone made it a rule that we could not raise money for these types of incidents, so we were told to never do it again. There was nothing unethical about it from my perspective, and in a pinch, I will do it again. I informed my staff, and I took full responsibility, but I will wallpaper my house with reprimands if it means helping others in need, especially my students. Just make sure your message, and expectation is that you want everything in the school done at the highest level of ethical behavior, including sports. If anything will have your character or integrity questioned, it will be athletics. Earlier I told you about my experience in high school, being recruited to play at a private school. Of course, when you are young, you have no idea what is going on, you just go play for another team. If you have children who play competitive sports then you already know how serious some people can take it, and you no doubt have already seen how unethical some can be to win.

**Courage Under Fire:** As the Executive Principal of a school you need to know that you will be required to have courage under circumstances that may cause you to question others, especially if you are working in a school serving the same demographic as Stratford STEM School. Students who live in poverty are automatically facing odds that sometimes seem insurmountable, and you are going to have to be very creative, and courageous with how you inspire, defend and hold accountable those children who have very little at home and not much to look forward to.

Sometimes it seems that all I do is defend and protect my students from all sorts of unacceptable influences, which sometimes includes those who should be embracing them instead of always assuming the negative. During the 2016 - 2017 school year, we lost four students, two to natural causes, that would have most likely been prevented had they had better insurance and medical care, and we also lost two other students to gun violence. Although I am thankful that none of these incidents occurred at school, when we love students and treat them like they are a part of your family, it hurts none the less. I'll never forget sitting at home and receiving a call that one of our students had been killed. As the details started to emerge, I was shocked. As a former law enforcement officer, I had witnessed just about anything you can imagine, and seen the worst this world can offer, but I had never seen anything like this before. One day after school, one of our young ladies was playing basketball outside when a man, known to her, came straight up to her and shot her numerous times. Yes, there are many more details, but I don't want to get into that. But, she was assassinated in broad daylight, and in all my time, I've never seen anything like it. She was an amazing young lady, loved and admired by all, and now, she's gone. Principals and leaders, you need to speak out when you see such things in your school, organization and community. It's easy to have courage when there is nothing at risk. Be that person who will do what is right, because it is right without hesitation.

**Communication:** The best communicators are the best listeners, but it does not stop there. Yes, your team loves it when you listen to them, but the majority of the time they also want constructive and supportive feedback. The exceptional principal communicates well with everyone, no matter what the circumstance or background of the other person. Exceptional principals need to be very focused and intentional about their communication with others. Every school has that quiet teacher, student or parent that never says much to anyone. They just go about their day, but never really communicate with many people. This does not mean that they don't want to communicate. I make sure to say hello to every teacher, student, and parent I encounter, so yes, I say hello a lot, and every day. How many times have you heard about the principal who walks down the hall and says nothing, to no one? The message here is that she/he does not care because they don't even acknowledge you. OoRah Leadership requires you to be purposeful about your interactions with everyone, and although they are not always going to be amazing connections, you can at least go into the interaction hoping for an amazing connection, it's all about your mindset.

I pride myself on being a great communicator, especially with angry parents. They come in so angry and ready to fight for their child, even though they know their child was wrong. I've always been successful dealing with conflict resolution, but from time-to-time, parents do not want to hear about my OoRah Leadership or accentuating the positive, they just want to fuss at you. Remember my assistant principal, Dr. Jones? I love when he is in a parent conference with me, especially when it is clear that I am not making any progress, and the level of anger has not changed. I wait for it, and I know it's coming, because Dr. Jones has a great understanding of when I've tried everything, and he comes into the conversation at just the right time. He and I work so well together, that we understand when we need support from each other, because we are so intentional about our communication. Let me tell you Dr. Jones's secret for de-escalating angry parents. He says, "Ma'am or sir, I have six kids, so I know what you must be thinking, because six kids are a lot." When he tells parents that he has six school-aged children they almost feel sorry for him and down comes the anger. Don't get me wrong,

He also has some very brilliant insight to poverty and parental concerns, but he uses that line every time, and it works. Exceptional Principals, and for those of you who want to be exceptional, outstanding communication skills are not something you attain, and then retain, you must work daily and hourly to maintain outstanding communications skills. Practice listening to others, and remind yourself not to respond until you have genuinely heard what that other person is saying. This is especially critical when you are speaking with your students. Give them time, all the time they need, and stop thinking about all you need to say or get accomplished.

**Relationships:** If you ask a room of educational leaders how important relationship building is, they will all raise their hands and agree that relationship building is vital to success with students. The interesting thing about relationship building is that most school leaders do not know how to do it. I keep referring to knowing yourself before you can truly understand what OoRah Leadership is, but it is crucial that we know ourselves before attempting to mentor or create relationships with others. If you are struggling in this area, I highly recommend that you look at yourself, because I promise you, you are the cause of any issues you are having. I'm not just talking about professional problems either; the same applies to any of your personal issues as well. The truth is, many leaders know their short comings already, and are either too scared to make the effort, or they just don't want to change. Unfortunately, some of these leaders work in our schools. As I sit here, I'm trying so hard to think of one great example to write about, but there are so many students and staff going through my head, and I'm finding it difficult to pick just one. Amazing relationships with my students is obviously one of my priorities, and I spend an intentional amount of time working on those relationships. There is one young man I want to mention is this book, because he has overcome so much, and I love him. He and his family have blessed our lives in so many ways. Our students are special, but let's face it, unique and lasting relationships must be forged, and my experience with this young man was a defining moment in my career. At the beginning of my second year at Stratford, I was so excited to see my students return from their summer break. That first day, I walked into every single classroom and spent about five minutes just fellowshipping with our students. I'll never forget walking into our life skills classroom and meeting a very special young man. He was a quiet young man, very friendly, and spoke with an obvious impediment. After I introduced myself, he said, "Hello, Dr. Stweele." Yes, I spelled it correct, remember his speech impediment. He was very articulate, but basically, he spoke with a slight lisp. The entire time we were talking I couldn't help but wonder why he was in a life skills classroom. Children who are in life skills are typically your most severe students who are learning how to care for themselves in the hopes that they could be self-sufficient one day. This young man was walking fine, spoke well, and seemed highly intelligent, so my curiosity continued to grow. I went back to my office, and called a meeting with his guidance counselor, and one of his teachers. Both told me that his individual education plan (IEP) required him to be in life skills. I was not at all satisfied with the idea that this incredible young man would spend his entire high school career in a class that would not give him more opportunities or push him to grow, so I called his grandparents, and requested a meeting. Now, this young man lived with his grandparents, because his mother and father did not fulfill their responsibility to their child, which we see all too often in our schools. His grandparents are exceptional people, and over the years, we have become very close friends. The following day we met, and I shared my concerns with his grandparents, and I suggested that we change his IEP and place him in a regular educational setting. The grandparents did not hesitate for one moment, and they were actually very excited that I called the meeting. The grandfather told me that he had always wanted his grandson in regular classes, but other principals would not allow it. So, with their permission, we changed the IEP and got him started in our criminal justice pathway. This young man's life was about to change in a drastic way, and I knew he could be successful if we just stayed purposeful about his future. All too often, children are dismissed, and we can't allow ourselves to dismiss any child, no matter what the circumstances. We are charged with a greater responsibility to be courageous and fight for all children, not just the ones who make our lives easier.

The following day we got him started in our criminal justice pathway, and I walked him down, and introduced him to our criminal justice teacher. Now, my criminal teacher was a former Marine and retired Federal Bureau of Investigations (FBI) agent. He only had one way, and that was his way. The three of us talked for a few moments, and I'll never forget when my teacher asked this young man a question, and he simply said, "No." My teacher said, "Look young man, if you're going to be in my classroom then "no" won't cut it. It's either "no sir, or yes sir" am I clear? He looked terrified, but he said, "Yes Sir." A few days later, this young man came to my office, and told me that another boy was bullying him. I know he wasn't used to other students picking on him or making fun of his lisp, and it bothered him. I said, "Do you want to know why that boy is picking on you? It's because you are not drinking your milk or doing your pushups every night. You have to start taking better care of yourself. Drink your milk and do 100 pushups every night." As soon as he left my office, I called his grandfather and explained our meeting. His grandfather also served in the military, and knew exactly what I was trying to do. The last thing this boy needed was for me to baby him, and to start working out all his problems. He already had the deck stacked against him, and what he needed was someone who loved him enough to let him go out and learn how to stand up for himself. He also needed to feel confident about himself, and to know what that feels like. A few weeks later he came into my office, and told me that every night he drank a glass of milk and did his pushups. He was so proud of himself; you could see it on his face. I said, "You still look scrawny, so make sure you are eating a lot and start doing 150 pushups every night." I was blown away when he said with a huge smile on his face, "Dr. Stweele, I'm not scrawny, and one day I'll be as big as you." I got up out of my seat and gave him a hug, and we both laughed a bit, and off he went, back out into high school halls that can sometimes be mean. For those of you who know me, I'm certain you can imagine this all playing out, and I hope you are laughing. I love children, and I will protect them with my life, but I do everything in my power to always be intentional with them, and never, ever, betray them.

As time went on, this young man flourished, and even joined our cadet corps, and mock trial team. One day, I was in a meeting with about twenty business partners when my door opened. It was my new friend, and two other students in full cadet corps uniforms. He walked into my office and said, "Dr. Stweele, you are under arrest, and I need to take you to trial right now." I had no idea this was going to happen, neither did my visitors. So, I was handcuffed and escorted to our mock courtroom for trial, and guess who was the prosecuting attorney? What was amazing was all my visitors came to watch this mock trial, and they stayed the entire time. He did his best to convict me of bank robbery, but the judge, who was actually his grandfather declared a mistrial, so I was set free. Of course, I never let him forget that he did not have what it takes to convict me, and to this day, we talk about that experience. We all loved watching him grow into a normal and happy student. He thrived on challenges, competition and loved being "one of the guys," and we did everything in our power to make sure he felt that way. One day, he walked into my office, shut the door, and said, "Dr. Stweele, I have a question for you. Can I please take your daughter to the prom?" I said, "Thank you for asking me, and if she says, yes, then you have my blessing to take her to the prom." A few hours later he returned, and said, "She said yes!" He was so excited, and so was I. One of the proudest moments of my life was learning that my daughter said, "Yes" to his invitation. He then said, "Dr. Stweele, I have one more thing to ask you. Can you please drive us to the prom?" We both laughed, and he left my office elated to just be normal, and loved. I have no idea what would have happened to him had we left him in life skills class, and not challenged him to be better. That same year, he graduated from high school with a regular educational diploma, and went to the Law Enforcement Academy at Nashville State Community College. He currently has a full-time security job with a very respectable agency, and has even been promoted. He is making his dreams come true, and he still calls me every now and then to see how I'm doing. He and I will stay life-long friends. Powerful and meaningful relationships only happen when our intent is blameless, and our actions are purposeful. I could have accepted the fact that this young man was placed in a certain class, and just moved on, but I would have been incredibly wrong for not having the courage, and integrity to do what was right… always do what is right.

**Love & Discipline:** Love and discipline, now this is where most people really get it wrong, especially school leaders and parents. When I first arrived at Stratford, I learned that in the previous year there had been some sixty-eight physical arrests. I'm talking about when our School Resource Officers are so overwhelmed they call for back up, and in just minutes there are five police cars at the school arresting young people. In my first year, and throughout the last seven years, we have never had a situation where our School Resource Officers called another police officer to come assist…never. Again, this is not just about me, it's about OoRah Leadership, or living your life in a purposeful and meaningful way, that truly allows you to change the landscape of a school, or your family.

I've attended numerous meetings and trainings on "restorative practices", and every time I leave, I'm more confused and disappointed that the training and philosophy is wrong. Like many districts, our district has always tried to reduce the number of discipline referrals, and or discipline issues in the schools. This is obviously a good endeavor, but if you are only trying to reduce the numbers, without a realistic approach to helping with issues of discipline, then you are only putting a band aide on the problem. A while back, one of our district supervisors asked me what I did to have such a drastic change on the culture at Stratford. He went on to ask me what my plan for the coming year was to reduce the number of discipline referrals. I told him that I did not have a plan to reduce referrals, and that I thought it was a mistake to make schools reduce referrals. I went on to say that we should see an increase in referrals if we are doing it right. He looked at me with this confused face, and said, "How does increasing referrals help the school?" Think about it, just take a moment and think about it. The reason parents have issues with their children, is they don't spend enough time with them, interacting with them, disciplining them, loving them. You must be intentional about your interaction with your children, and being in a school is no different. My wife and I have four children ranging in age from twenty-eight to eleven. Every time one of my children enters the room, I make every effort to acknowledge them. Nowadays, when our eleven-year-old daughter enters the room, I say, "Hey, beauty" or something that makes her smile. Don't get me wrong, when they deserved attention regarding discipline they received it as well, and you must understand that discipline is one of the greatest examples of love you can give your children or students. You must be intentional, and you must look forward to those times when you can discipline your children and students. The reason I don't care about the increase of referrals is because it gives you more opportunities to counsel and demonstrate your love for your students. If parents who have children that are undisciplined, and are going down the wrong path would understand accountability and restoration, will solve most of their problems. The same applies with your students. You don't have to work every referral, and put it in the database, but every referral should be an amazing opportunity for you to impact a student in a profound way. Discipline is an essential part of demonstrating love for children. Make sure you and your team are consistent at all cost. When your students and staff know that the discipline policies are going to be consistent, and that you are going to be consistent, you will start seeing things rapidly change, and you will quickly realize that your students and staff want loving accountability.

**Compassion:** There is never a time where your compassion is a weakness. Even if you make a decision based solely on compassion and it turns out to be the wrong choice, it is still not a weakness. Compassion sometimes requires a great awareness of who you are. Compassion is not feeling sorry for someone, it is a verb, and it requires action. Feeling sorry for someone or wishing their life was better is not a demonstration of compassion. A compassionate person will not only feel sorrow, but will take action to demonstrate love and understanding of what someone may be going through. Take action when you see others suffering. Be genuine, intentional and make sure you do not miss those amazing opportunities to not only help, but inspire as well. OoRah Leaders are courageous, and they don't consider their own egos, especially when it comes to caring for others.

**Mission Minded:** The mission matters, so don't ever lose sight of that. Yes, I want you to be the very best OoRah Leader you can be, and that comes with a significant understanding of yourself and others, but I do not want to send the message that the mission is less important. If you are doing it right, and I hope you do, the mission is always at the forefront of why you are leading with OoRah Leadership. You must, however, be very aware of where your followers are on the mission, and their understanding of the mission. They don't always have to know every aspect, but if they trust your leadership, they will not have to know, they will just trust you. Trust is an interesting word, because truly we are all going to be let down from time-to-time from someone we thought we could trust. It may not be intentional, but it will happen. You can build a level of trust with your followers if you hold yourself accountable enough to care about them, and lead them on a mission of excellence, success, happiness, and peace.

**Sacrifice:** OoRah Leadership requires a level of sacrifice unlike anything you have ever experienced. As many of you already know, being an educator and especially a principal requires a lot of sacrifice. Sacrifice from your families, friends, and hobbies. There are evening and weekend obligations, and don't forget about athletics which keeps me away from home during the year several nights per week. It does feel great to sacrifice for such an amazing cause, but let me be clear, OoRah Leadership takes sacrifice to another level. Your staff, students, and employees deserve someone who is willing to sacrifice for the mission, and for the team. They deserve someone who will not only lead by example, but will demonstrate what hard work and sacrifice looks like.

**Visible & Available:** I've heard people talk about their "Open door policy", but when it comes time to find them or get their attention they are nowhere to be found. OoRah Leaders, make time to be in the halls, interact with as many people as possible, and not make excuses for why they don't. My office door stays open, literally 99% of the time. The only time my door is closed is when I'm in a confidential meeting with a parent, teacher or student. I do not close my door for any other reason, and my staff and students know this. Every day, without exception, I will be in a conversation with a teacher, or parent, and a student will just walk up to my door, and look in to see if I'm here. They always apologize for interrupting, but say they need to speak with me. Exceptional principals never allow a student who says, "I need to talk to you" to walk away no matter what. Every meeting, phone call or email can wait. A few years ago, the Mayor of Nashville was in my office with a few other elected officials. They were all waiting to go up to the library for some celebration. A student came to my door and interrupted, and I could tell from her face that she needed to speak with me. I stopped my conversation with everyone in my office and excused myself to make sure my student was ok. This happens every day, to all of us, but far too often, leaders dismiss the urgency of a student or parent needing support, and accidentally or intentionally never meet their needs.

**Genuine:** Exceptional principals, make sure you are living your life in such a way that allows you to be genuine. If you are struggling with this, please make a significant effort to reinvent yourself. People, especially children know when you are not genuine, and when they know or think it, it makes relationship building impossible

## No Excuses, Only Results

Whenever you decide to reinvent yourself, your school or business, you need to be very clear that excuses are just that, and you should never allow them to become a part of your culture. Excuses should never be tolerated. When you make an excuse for yourself, or your organization you are setting yourself up for unlimited failure and you start to narrow your options for success. Excuses are a psychological phenomenon that helps us reduce stress and anxiety by categorizing our reasons for failure. When you make an excuse for why you were not successful, or why it did not go your way, the chances are that you already pre-established your excuses before beginning your new mission. I know, I'll wait until New Year's Day to start eating right or exercising. I can't work out because I have too much work, or I will miss time with the kids. I can't go back to school because I won't have time for my job. If I had a quarter for every time I've heard parents use their children as an excuse, I could retire now. Remember when I told you about the administrator who said, "These kids can't do this work."

A short time ago one of our wonderful students was shot and killed while playing basketball in broad day light. A few weeks after her death, I attended a community meeting on crime and violence in her neighborhood. I sat there and listened to more and more talk about how this program or that program would help. The police representatives pleaded with the crowd that they needed more people willing to call when they see suspicious activity. After the officer's plea, someone said, "The community if afraid, and traumatized. Their learned behavior is to not trust." This is what I'm talking about regarding excuses. If you want to transform your school or neighborhood then you need to stop making excuses and stand up for what is good, fair, and blameless. Stop telling people why you can't get something done, and why you can't be successful. If you are giving up, then there is no place for OoRah Leadership in your life.

    We do not allow students at Stratford to make excuses about their home life or upbringing, we expect, no we demand respect, and effort. Yes, we do understand their plight in life, and how difficult it may be at times, but we tolerate no excuses for failure, and neither should you. Never allow excuses to keep you from the responsibility you have not only to yourself, but to others as well, and I promise you, as soon as you quit making excuses for yourself, it becomes much easier to not accept them from others. Probably the thing that frustrates me the most is when a teacher comes to my office with excuse after excuse about why their day was so horrible, and how one or two students ruined their entire day. Let me be very clear on this point, if you are evaluating your happiness, success or peace on a few individuals, you have problems of your own that need to be resolved, it's not your students, or colleagues fault.

    In early 2017, I did some training for a school in West Tennessee. I call this training OoRah Leadership, because it focuses on you, and how to be a powerful influencer and leader of others. As a motivational speaker, I am always reading the crowd to make sure everyone is engaged, and that they are listening intently. During this training I noticed a lady listening, but you could tell that she was not really feeling the message of hope, transformation and no excuses. She waited for a few hours, and just before lunch, raised her hand with a question. When I acknowledged her, she went on for several minutes about how others had mistreated her, and how she had volunteered for a specific coaching position. I was still waiting for the question, but she went on and on. At one point she even put the school's principal, who was sitting a few seats away on notice that he had treated her wrongly. She finally got around to asking her question. She said, "How am I supposed to motivate myself and inspire others, if no one is motivating or inspiring me?" Of course, throughout her comments, and eventually her questions, her colleagues were sitting patiently, but it was obvious that they were not only disappointed in her behavior, and lack of professionalism, but they were not at all surprised. Although I was not impressed with her demeanor or intent, I know her question was genuine, and she honestly wanted to know why she should care, if others did not care about her. I think this is a very real and fundamental question that many ask themselves every day. Why should I get up, go to work with people who do not care about me, and try if I know it will not be rewarded? Feels that way sometimes, and for some, their entire life is spent questioning, defending and making excuses for themselves.

When you are in a situation like this, and you know that you are being put on the "hot seat", you need to make sure you slow down, and offer a well thought out response. Keep in mind, that most of the time, when you are communicating with negative people, your response will not satisfy them, it will simply offer them more excuses for why they are unhappy. Following her question, I paused for a few moments, and I was transparent about it. I explained to the entire room that I wanted to take a moment to reflect on the question. I did this for a few different reasons, mostly to reflect on the question, but I also did it to demonstrate a willingness to answer a challenging question from a challenging person. I also, did not want to miss the opportunity to possibly help in this situation, but to also educate others in the room. I replied to her question by saying, "When did you ask for this position, and when you received a response, did you go speak with your principals?" She said, "I knew it was going to happen, so I did not go ask why it was not approved." It was obvious that it was not the time or place to continue this dialogue, so we broke for lunch, and moved on with the day.

 A few months later, and at the request of the administration, I returned to the school and conducted an analysis of the entire operation from instruction to moral. Later that same afternoon Dr. Jones and I met with all the teachers in small groups. During our meeting with this very teacher, she asked me rather abruptly about why I did not answer her question months prior, and what I thought about her. Friends, I've learned many times over the years that being rude to someone is never a good idea, even though I know we all want to be occasionally. We all get frustrated with people, but in general, it is not wise to be rude, and I never intend to be rude or hurt feelings, but there is an appropriate time to be honest with people about how they are interfering with their own lack of success or happiness. Following her question, I said, "Do you really want to know what I'm thinking, and do you want me to share that with the group. We can talk privately if you wish." She said, "No, go ahead, I'm good either way." I said, "Very well. Your attitude and general outlook on life is hurting your chances for future opportunities. You were unprofessional a few months ago when you called out your principal in front of everyone, and your demeanor now is rude, but you already know that, and yet you continue without thinking about changing. You also need to know that not only is this my observation, this is also the observation of many of your peers, and they like you, and want you to be happy and successful." I would like to say that after a few weeks this teacher called me and apologized, or had some sort of epiphany but that did not happen. She did however email me, explaining that she had God and if God loved her then she was not changing anything about herself. Of course, it has and still never ceases to amaze me how some people use God to defend their actions, or rationalize their unwillingness to change. Ultimately, and no matter what your reason, happiness, peace, and that feeling of worth is up to you, not your boss, wife, husband or money, but entirely up to you, and I hope you find all of it.

## Final Thoughts...For Now

What is holding you back from success, from happiness, from peace? What is keeping you from being an outstanding leader, a leader who people trust, respect, and proudly serve. What is stopping you from OoRah leadership? I have been fortunate to be able to speak at conferences all over the world. Mostly, I speak about leadership, emotional intelligence, communication skills, things that will help people and organizations grow. In May of 2017, I spoke on OoRah Leadership at the Minority Leadership Conference in Bay St. Louis, Mississippi. It was an amazing conference and Mississippi is a beautiful place. During my presentation I always challenge my audience to do one simple thing that will help them be confronted with their own level of leadership. I want you also to try it, and really take a close look at not only your apprehension, but the response you are sure to receive:

### The First Mission

I want you to write out a personal mission statement that reflects your mission in life. It can be whatever you would like, but it must detail what you want others to know about you if they were to read it. When you have accomplished this, and it shouldn't take you that long to write down a few lines or a paragraph perhaps, but when you are done, post it for the world to see, or at least put in on the refrigerator. I want you to understand the psychology that is taking place here, so you will learn more about yourself, and what you are comfortable doing, and what makes you uncomfortable. Many people in leadership roles are uncomfortable with being vulnerable, or the perception that they are weak. I understand, but will submit that is an error in judgement for your leadership potential. Think about how many times you must write this mission statement, and how many times you think about what others will think, and then sit back and wait for the responses to come in. The responses will vary, mostly because people will then be confronted with their response, so most will only say something like, "That is awesome" or "Good job." Very few will describe what they are feeling in detail, because again, they too are nervous about the reaction of others. I challenge you to try this, and explore, and examine the truth about how it makes you feel, being honest with yourself in the hopes that you will continue to grow. Another aspect of this very simple mission is to announce in writing that you want to be on this mission, and although you may not be entirely now, it is your desire to do so. For example, I want to be a great husband, and father, so I say it, and I wrote it down. Now, when I display it for others to see, it gives it so much more meaning because now I have others also holding me accountable.

 If you have the courage, try this tonight, and remember excuses are not compatible with excellence. Tell your family you want to have a "Family meeting." Make sure you say, "family meeting." If you have no children, then it's just you and your spouse. If you are single, ask a friend or relative. When everyone is convened explain to them that you called the meeting to express to them your mission statement. Tell them that you want them to know how you want to live your life, and where you need support. Do this as a family, and have everyone write it down, and put it on the fridge. It's so simple, and so powerful. The sad part is, most will not do it, for various reasons, but mostly because they are embarrassed, and don't want to be committed to what they wrote down. Personally, I'm proud that I want to be a great husband, father, brother, and friend. I want everyone to know that, and if I fall short now and then, I'm sorry, and want to be held accountable.

### The second mission

A similar experience, but I want you to call someone or speak with someone in person that you really care about, and perhaps love, but for whatever reason you have not expressed that appreciation or love in a while. Call them or tell them how much they mean to you, and be specific. It could sound something like this, "Hi this is your brother, and I just wanted to tell you how much I love you, and I wish I told you more often, but I was thinking about you today, and wanted you to know that." Wow, even now many of you reading this are already uncomfortable with the experience, while others are saying this is easy.

Think about the power and growth it takes to be intentional about your actions. Many of you will receive a response of, "What's wrong, is everything ok." I would consider that a normal response, but interesting to say the least. How many times in the past few weeks have you thought about telling someone you love them, but haven't? How many times have you wanted to tell a co-worker that you appreciate them, and think they are awesome, but you didn't? Why? What is holding you back from being the leader, husband, wife, employer or employee that you want to be?

When I first finished my master's degree in psychology and counseling, I worked part-time for a counseling group in Orlando, Florida, and then had my own practice for a while. The majority of my clients were seeking enlightenment about life mostly. Every once in a while, I would treat a client with depression, anxiety, marital problems, but mostly I counseled my clients on making great decisions, and helping them realize how their choices were negatively impacting their lives. I'll never forget this one couple; they had been married for nearly twenty years. They were seeking counseling because the husband enjoyed hanging out with his friends, which included going out to night clubs every now and then. The wife was not happy for many reasons, but mostly because her husband was hanging out in night clubs with his buddies, and she knew that nothing good could come from that. One night, he came home with lipstick on his collar, and it got serious then. I remember asking about the marriage, and both replied that the marriage was excellent except for "guy's night out." Both said they loved each other, and of course he said they were just dancing, nothing happened. Finally, he asked me what he should do, and I said, "Do you love your wife? Do you want to stay happily married? Do you value her?" When he said, "Yes," I said, "Well, stop going out with the guys to bars and nightclubs." It's not brain surgery, and it's rather simple. If he truly wants the things he said, he has the answer in front of him. You can't value your wife, and then go out to nightclubs with your friends. You can fool yourself if you want, but the truth is absolute. This is only one example of thousands where leaders fail themselves, and in so doing, fail others. The vast majority of the time we already know the answers to the most difficult questions, but often we don't have the character or integrity to make the right choice. We must get to a place within ourselves where making the right choice, because it is right, honest and blameless comes naturally, and represents who we want to be, and who we want others to see. When you value something, I mean truly value something, it's amazing how much effort you will put into keeping or maintaining it. I value my wife, my family, my staff, students and community. I value each of them so much that I am intentional about how I conduct myself always. Yes, I value each of them differently, but in some respect the same. I love all of them, even though some are easier to love than others, but if I'm going to value them, I need to be able to love each of them even when it is not easy. I do everything in my power to protect each of them, and if you are a principal, or ever want to be a principal then you should know right off, it is not easy to protect your students and staff all the time. You are not always going to be able to save them, protect them or see them be successful, but if you know that you are giving everything you have, you are sacrificing for the hope of others, then you can rest easy, and know that you are genuine, and blameless in your pursuit of OoRah Leadership.

From time-to-time we are all capable of being selfish, demanding, rude, and ignorant. We are capable of hurting others, and only considering ourselves. These are some of the things that we try or should try to eliminate while on our journey to live as blameless as possible. What moves you? What stops you in your tracks and makes you contemplate how you are living your life, or what you might need to change? I make every effort to be confronted with how I can be better in all walks of life. You might think that it monopolizes my time, and stresses me out, but it doesn't, it gives me energy and meaning to always want to excel. So, what is keeping you from living the life you want, and realizing the dreams you have? Why haven't you found success in your leadership, and with your team?

  Leadership, authentic leadership, OoRah Leadership, cares more about others than anything else. It does not allow for a mindset of personal gain, and only seeks to motivate and inspire others toward a greater goal of accomplishing the mission. We all have a mission, and sometimes that mission is lost because we don't put the team first. No mission will ever get accomplished by yourself, and the team is the only way you will succeed, at home, or at work. Yes, you may find success in your silo, but you will be there alone, and, being alone is mission failure. You see this across the board in organizations, schools, hospitals, you name it. When those in leadership positions care more about themselves than those they lead, you can almost certainly see the lack of vision and excellence they portray. On the other hand, when you lead with a compelling passion for others, and you express your desire to lead with integrity, honor, and courage, you will not only find excellence in your life, but you will also foster profound and purposeful teams that can conquer any mission. What mission are you on? Do you want to change your business, school or team? Do you want to find joy, happiness and laughter in your relationships? I tell my staff and students all the time that the journey of life is a short one, and living it to the fullest every day is worthwhile, but taking the easy road or the unethical road leads to personal disappointment, and despair. Humble yourself, and identify who you are. If you are having trouble with this concept, ask someone close to you to help you, or call me, and I will be glad to help. It can be your spouse, but keep in mind that your spouse is most likely going to sugar coat it. Find a colleague or counselor, and find out who you are. This is not always an effortless process, and the truth is sometimes difficult to acknowledge, but the only way you can move forward is to be honest with yourself. If you want to be a better father, then do it. If you want to be a better husband, boss or friend…do it, and stop making excuses for why you are not finding peace and joy in your life.

OoRah Leadership was something I made up, because I love the Marine Corps, and am so thankful for what I learned, and how I was inspired during my service. Call your leadership whatever you want, but remember that excuses are incompatible with excellence. You don't have time to be lazy, unethical, or mean. Your family, friends, and co-workers need for you to be the person you want to be. They need for you to be highly motivated, and truly dedicated to them, and their future. If the team fails, it's because you failed them. If the team succeeds, it's because you did not get their way, and led with a compelling vision, and a true passion for them, and the success of the mission. I trust and pray that you have been motivated and confronted with what is keeping you from happiness and success. Until the next mission………. OoRah and Semper Fi, friends…

Me and my youngest, Ella Grace….my beauty.

Be intentional and purposeful about loving others. God bless you on your journey of excellence.